Shaman Pathways

... an ever-growing library of shared knowledge

Aubry's Dog, Me
A practical and essential guid
energi

T0159488

Black Horse White Horse, Melusine Draco
Feel the power and freedom as Black Horse, White Horse
guides you down the magical path of this most noble animal

Celtic Chakras, Elen Sentier
Tread the British native shaman's path, explore the Goddess
hidden in the ancient stories; walk the Celtic chakra spiral
labyrinth

Druid Shaman, Danu Forest
A practical guide to Celtic shamanism with exercises and
techniques as well as traditional lore for exploring the Celtic
Otherworld

Elen of the Ways, Elen Sentier
British shamanism has largely been forgotten: the reindeer
Goddess of the ancient Boreal forest is shrouded in mystery ...
follow her deer-trods to rediscover her old ways

Following the Deer Trods, Elen Sentier
A practical handbook for anyone wanting to begin the old
British paths. Follows on from *Elen of the Ways*

Trees of the Goddess, Elen Sentier
Work with the trees of the Goddess and the old ways of Britain

Way of the Faery Shaman, Flavia Kate Peters
Your practical insight into Faeries and the elements they engage
to unlock real magic that is waiting to help you

Web of Life, Yvonne Ryves
A new approach to using ancient ways in these contemporary
and often challenging times to weave your life path

What people are saying about

Shaman Pathways – Deathwalking

Deathwalking is a brilliant and much needed anthology on the topic of death. The collection of authors who work with different spiritual traditions provide multiple views on assisting deceased spirits return to Source. The collection of perspectives and ways of working to help the deceased are fascinating and educational. **Sandra Ingerman**, MA, author of *Soul Retrieval* and *Walking in Light: The Everyday Empowerment of Shamanic Life*

Our ancestors knew death intimately – recognizing it as an integral part of life. They tended the dying and prepared the bodies of loved ones who had passed. Yet, even with this kind of death-midwifery, some of the dead would linger in our world. Especially those who had died suddenly, were attached to people or places, were uncertain of their worthiness to pass into a "good" place or who died under horrific circumstances, were likely to remain as lost and wandering spirits.

Today, we live in a world of disconnection and dissociation from much of life and certainly from death. This anthology offers the first-person perspectives of contemporary practitioners who work with those who haven't made their complete transition from the world of the living. *Shaman Pathways Deathwalking: Helping Them Cross the Bridge* is a rare opportunity to learn more about guiding souls and also about the compassionate people who perform this essential service.
Evelyn C. Rysdyk, internationally recognized shamanic practitioner, teacher, and best-selling author whose titles include *The Norse Shaman* and *Spirit Walking: A Course In Shamanic Power*

In the modern Western world we tend to avoid all mention of death, viewing it with fear rather than as a natural part of life.

Even with the current resurgence in shamanism, psychopomp work (deathwalking) remains a practice rarely written about which is where this anthology comes in as a valuable resource. With its rich sharing of original experiences and knowledge from individual authors, including traditional rituals and mythology as well as a generous sharing of personal moving stories of bereavement and spirit work, *Deathwalking* provides a diversity of ideas and information for us to consider as well as being a wonderful tribute to those who went before us.

June Kent, Editor, *Indie Shaman* magazine

When I was two and a half I found my mother hanging from the chandelier. She had been at Pearl Harbor and suffered what would now be called PTSD. My family's way of dealing with this was to bury it, and deny it ever happened. All they ever said was, she got sick and died. But, I had been there, had experienced the trauma and heard the screams of my grandmother. Had there been information like that which Imelda Almqvist and her fellow contributors offer, I could have avoided many years of therapy and much suffering. We must learn to teach parents how to support their children in dealing with death so it can become a lesson for how to live a precious and more meaningful life of love, kindness, courage and compassion. I think this kind of work is among the most important of our time.

Michael Stone, teacher, writer, shamanic practitioner, and host and producer of KVMR's *Conversations* and the Shift Network's *Shamanism Global Summit*

The rituals of death impact us throughout life. This collection of essays expresses the importance of deathwalking, and how the way we honor death informs how we can best live.

S. Kelley Harrell, author of *Teen Spirit Guide to Modern Shamanism*

SHAMAN PATHWAYS

Deathwalking

Helping Them Cross the Bridge

Shaman Pathways

Deathwalking

Helping Them Cross the Bridge

Edited by Laura Perry

MOON
BOOKS

Winchester, UK
Washington, USA

First published by Moon Books, 2018
Moon Books is an imprint of John Hunt Publishing Ltd., No. 3 East Street, Alresford
Hampshire SO24 9EE, UK
office1@jhpbooks.net
www.johnhuntpublishing.com
www.moon-books.net

For distributor details and how to order please visit the 'Ordering' section on our website.

Text copyright: Laura Perry 2017

ISBN: 978 1 78535 818 0
978 1 78535 819 7 (ebook)
Library of Congress Control Number: 2017962230

A CIP catalogue record for this book is available from the British Library.

Design: Stuart Davies

Printed and bound by CPI Group (UK) Ltd, Croydon, CR0 4YY, UK

We operate a distinctive and ethical publishing philosophy in
all areas of our business, from our global network of authors to
production and worldwide distribution.

Contents

Foreword 1

Acknowledgments 9

Introduction 10

Psychopomps and Psychopaths: Children in the role of psychopomp or soul conductor – Imelda Almqvist 12

Midwife to the Dying: The Post-Tribal Shaman's Role – Kenn Day 19

Deathwalking with the Living: A shamanic healer's perspective – Yvonne Ryves 26

Reality, Spirit, and Death – Elen Sentier 31

Deathwalking with Reluctant Spirits – Dorothy Abrams 38

Hindu Last Rites – Vani Neelakantan 45

Dealing with Misplaced Energy: Examples and practices – Janet Elizabeth Gale 50

Deathwalking: Three encounters with death – Lucya Starza 57

A Path of Song, a Path of Light: Guiding the dead in the Celtic traditions – Danu Forest 62

The How Not to Do It Chapter – Laura Perry 68

Foreword

Because of their familiarity with the spirit world, shamans are called upon in traditional societies to assist the souls of those in the process of dying to move on into the next world gracefully, cleanly, and without problems. They may also intervene in other circumstances when the dead become trapped or lost or are in some way troublesome to the village. It is rare in the modern world for a shaman to be asked to perform these duties (though it does happen). He or she may, however, be commissioned to work in a similar field – that of hauntings (typically of a property) or the removal of negative forces or realignment of energies within a house or workplace. This is the shaman acting as psychopomp or, as this book describes, as a deathwalker.

Shamans developed these skills (or so the story goes) because in traditional cultures it was noticed that when people died, especially in sudden or violent circumstances, there was a tendency for their spirits to hang around. For example, after a battle with a rival tribe, a village might experience unusual phenomena – the failure of crops, children having bad dreams, people seeing phantoms or strange lights and movements around them, and so on. The shaman would be sent on a journey to the spirit world to explore and find an explanation for these things and to resolve the situation if he could.

From such spiritual explorations and interventions, shamans have acquired knowledge of the Land of the Dead, the needs of the souls who occupy it, and the ways of helping them find peace beyond the human plane. Extrapolating from this, they also understand the need for people to die well, trouble-free, with all of their business in this world completed so that their experience of dying and of death will be peaceful and sacred and final.

In exploring the cosmology of the otherworld to understand

what happens after death, shamans discovered that when a person dies, his spirit moves from the world of everyday reality into what "core shamans" call "the middle world," the energetic dimension which is parallel to our own. (There is even some suggestion as to the weight of this soul: 21 grams, the amount that is mysteriously lost by the body at the point of death). The soul remains here for a brief time until it is contacted by the spirits of ancestors, angels, or allies who escort it to either the "upper" or "lower world" where it undergoes a life review, understands the lessons it came to Earth to learn, and begins to settle into its new discarnate state.

The difference between upper and lower world as a final destination for the soul has nothing to do with the Christianized conception of good and evil, by the way (you don't go "up to Heaven" if you have been "good" and "down to Hell" if you've been "bad"); it is merely a cultural convention. The shamans of different cultures believe that the Land of the Ancestors or the Dead is to be found in different places within the spiritual cosmology. In the Western world we tend to believe that the spirit first makes a horizontal transition from the ordinary middle world (the land of the living) to the spiritual middle world (the land of spirit or energy) and then a vertical transition upwards into the angelic realms (the upper world). In Haiti, by contrast, after the initial horizontal shift, the transition is downwards into the "land beneath the waters" where ancestral spirits reside. (And just to confound us all, those who have died in Irish myth are sometimes described as sailing away to the islands of the west, which is neither up nor down but across ...)

When this period of review and rebalancing is over, the soul may move on into the continuing process of life-death-rebirth or, in some cultures, if the soul is very evolved and the person has acted during life in accordance with the will of God (the love-energy of the universe) it has a choice to escape this process altogether and become one with God his/her/itself, going back to the universal pool of energy from whence it started. The Christian philosopher Teilhard de Chardin called this "merging with the 'Godhead'." Its parallel in the Buddhist tradition might be the bliss state of nirvana where we become like a "drop of water in an ocean," at one with everything. Some spirits choose to do so but others take pity on us because, having been human themselves, they recognize that being alive in this world is a difficult journey with sometimes hard lessons to learn and sorrows to bear. To support us they elect to become our helpers instead. These are our "allies," our "guardian angels" and the psychopomps in the spirit world with whom we work as deathwalkers in this one. Their names vary by culture. Anubis in Egypt, Charon to the Greeks, Shiva, Daena ... the Grim Reaper. All do the work of deliverance, comforting and escorting the newly-dead into their next adventures on their ways back to God after we have done our work of preparing the soul for death and comforting the still-living after the passage of their loved one is made.

We in the West know something of the stages of death from research that has been conducted into near-death experiences or NDEs. The pioneer of such research is Dr. Raymond Moody, who introduced the subject in his book *Life After Life* where he recorded the experiences of 150 people who had died temporarily and then been revived. There are, he says, a number of things that occur in every near-death experience:

1. A sensation of being out-of-body, rising up and floating above the physical self and looking down dispassionately at the "shell" of the body while the self they now occupy is experienced as lighter and less-constrained. This sensation may be accompanied by a strange sound, described as buzzing or ringing, and a feeling of deep peace and contentment.
2. A sensation of rushing quickly through a dark tunnel towards a source of light.

3. There is a meeting with wise and loving beings on the other side of the tunnel, entities that are perceived as the souls of relatives, friends or ancestors who are there to greet them.

4. There is then a period of orientation followed by a meeting with a spiritually powerful being who is understood to be the ruler of this realm and is sometimes described as God. This meeting inspires feelings of reverence and awe.

5. This being presents the dead person with a detailed review of all they have done in their lives so they relive it and see how their life has been part of an intricate pattern. There may be a feeling of karmic learning associated with this – not a punishment or making amends but an opportunity for wisdom to be received (like a debriefing on the life experience).

6. Those that undergo this review and are revived return with the knowledge that love is the most important thing in the world.

7. The emotions experienced in this otherworld are often so intense and beautiful that there is a reluctance to come back. The Supreme Being, however, will advise the dead person that he must return, that it is not his time; or sometimes will offer him a choice to go or stay. When they return, it is normally because the near-death-experiencer senses a need from loved ones who are still living and returns out of duty or compassion for them.

There are, of course, parallels with the "core shamanic" method of contacting spirits – the journey through a tunnel or up into the realm of sky beings to a spiritual landscape bathed in light; the out-of-body feeling of spirit flight; the meeting with guides and tutelary spirits who have an air of wisdom and compassion about them, and so on; giving some credence to the modern urban shaman's assertion that the shamanic journey is "not just imagination," but a true out-of-body experience taken into the world of spirit.

Pediatrician Melvin Morse offers us further evidence for what happens after death, having spent 30 years studying near-death experiences in children. In 1982, while working at a clinic in Idaho, he was called to a young girl who had drowned in a swimming pool and had no heartbeat for 19 minutes. Miraculously, he was able to revive her and she went on to recover. Strangely, however, although dead at the time, she could recount the details of her resuscitation and told doctors that while she was "away" she had been led through a tunnel to a place she called Heaven.

Intrigued, Morse began a study of near-death experiences with children at Seattle Children's Hospital, comparing the experiences of 26 who had been resuscitated after death with those of 131 who were severely ill and in intensive care but not near death. His results showed that 88% in the NDE group had undergone experiences consistent with those identified by Raymond Moody as the near-death archetype, while none of the other children had.

Morse followed this research with a long-term study of these children, observing their progress as they grew up, compared with a control group who had not had near-death experiences. His results show that the survivors of near-death experiences have a much enhanced and richer experience of living as well as an appreciation of the sacred and of compassion in daily life. Adult survivors of childhood near-death experiences are, for example, more likely to donate money to charity, to volunteer in the community, to work in the caring professions, to treat their bodies better, and are less likely to suffer from drug abuse or similar problems. "When we die, we become fully conscious, aware of our surroundings, and experience spiritual insights we do not often have at other times in our lives," says Morse. "We [also] learn that human beings have an under-used area of the brain which is responsible for spiritual intuitions, paranormal abilities such as telepathy and remote viewing, and the power to heal not only the soul, but the body as well."

From these accounts we understand that the world we pass on to is one of great beauty. Others tell us that this is particularly true in circumstances where the person has had an opportunity to adjust to their death and prepare for it. What shamans have discovered, though, is that when death is sudden, unexpected, or has fear and trauma associated with it (such as a murder, a war, or an accident) the person who has died can remain attached to the Earth because of the strong emotion that holds him there or because his death was so sudden that he literally does not know he has died.

Unfinished business is a major reason why spirits are unable to move on. In the sin eating tradition of Wales, for example, "sins" (things for which the person has not made amends) can become weights on the soul and these hold the spirit tied to the Earth. Another form of attachment is addiction. Where a person has been a drug addict or alcoholic, for example, it may be that their craving holds them here so they can vicariously enjoy their physical pleasures through another. This is one of the reasons for possession. It also accounts for the high rate of reported pub hauntings whereby spirits hang around the places they were able to drink and experience high emotions (in fact, every place associated with heightened emotion – a theater, cinema, castle, hospital, cemetery, hotel, and so on – is likely to have a higher chance of a haunting since the energies they contain draw the spirits to them).

In such situations of attachment the soul becomes confused, stuck, lost in the middle world or resistant to moving on. This is what shamans found when they set out to explore the reasons for post-tribal conflict in the example given earlier. It then became the job of the shaman to release these lost souls so that peace was restored to the village. To do so he would journey to find these souls and negotiate with them to move on. In this sense, psychopomp work is soul retrieval for the dead. It is an area where, in the modern West, at least, far more training is needed because, simply enough, more deathwalkers are required as so few of them exist or are engaged in this work, which is also why this is a much-needed book.

One very basic qualification for writing about deathwalking, I suppose, is that one has had some experience of death and paid attention to the curiosities and teachings surrounding it; better yet, that one has died and returned and can speak with first-hand authority. In 2016, within the space of three months, I died once and was on my way back there a further two times, having had three heart attacks (the first of which killed me for a little while) in rapid succession for reasons that no one, including my doctors, could understand. With the refreshing honesty of the medical profession in Spain, when asked why two of my arteries had, out of the blue, decided to collapse one after the other, they shrugged and said (with what seemed to be a degree of pride) *no se; puede haberle pasado a cualquiera* (no idea; could have happened to anyone).

The "near-death archetype" I described above leads us to believe that at such moments, during or immediately after our deaths, a purpose – to our lives, our experiences, our being here at all – will be revealed to us so that we find some meaning at last. This was not true in my case, however. No angels sang, no tunnels opened, no white lights shone, nor did a line of happy ancestors show up to welcome me home. My death just hurt and dragged on a bit and other than that, it was dull.

What was more interesting to me was how I changed as a result of my experience when I came back from death. Again, I did not follow the NDE archetype. I did not become more loving or compassionate as doctors Moody and Morse would have predicted (in fact, the opposite), but I did develop an almost x-ray vision or "spider sense" about people. Even more so than before, I needed only to look at them to know their stories, their patterns, their so-called "dis-eases," and how they (we, us) trivialized their lives and turned them into soap operas on endless repeat instead of engaging fully with them as something finite and wonderful.

I could tell people their entire history – from childhood trauma to how they were stuck right now – and they would absolutely agree and commit to do something about it and then, with few exceptions, the next day they would do something as stupid and self-defeating as before.

But we must hold on to hope that there is still possibility for these people – for us – and for change, because, well, what else do we have? Only hope and faith, but this is still enough to change worlds.

And so I hope this little book of death teaches you as much about the preciousness of your life as it helps you prepare for its passing, so that you get to spend your time here having the most amazing adventures and wasting not a second of it.

This is the final gift of the deathwalker, I think; it is not just that they aid the process of dying or help those who are dead to move forwards; it is that they can also help those who are living find a life of wonder and peace and joy.

Ross Heaven
November 2017
Spain

Ross is a shaman and healer and the author of almost 20 books on shamanism, healing, plant medicines and shamanic herbalism. He has a website at www.thefourgates.org where you can find out more and join his workshops.

Acknowledgments

A book like this takes a community to create, and I'm indebted to a whole host of people who have put their time and effort into this valuable resource. I'm grateful to all the Moon Books authors who were willing to share their experiences in deathwalking and psychopomp work, some of which are quite personal and moving. I'm also thankful for Imelda Almqvist and Yvonne Ryves, who rounded up some endorsements for us by contacting people I didn't know. Ross Heaven has graciously written a foreword that adds another dimension to the collection; I hope our lovely readers have ears to hear what he so eloquently says. And of course, Trevor Greenfield and the whole Moon Books staff have provided valuable support throughout the project. Finally, I must offer my heartfelt thanks to the wider shamanic community for sustaining the practice of deathwalking when it has largely been lost to mainstream Western society.

Introduction

Deathwalking. Psychopomping. You may not have heard these terms before you picked up this book, but they mean the same thing: helping the spirits of the deceased move on from this world to the next. This is a practice that goes back millennia, if not eons, but one that is barely known in mainstream modern Western society. Our culture puts a lot of effort into keeping people alive but then many of us are left not knowing what to do when a loved one passes on, or when a natural disaster occurs and hundreds or thousands of people die. What happens to their souls? Can they find their way to wherever they belong on their own or do they need help? As it happens, many of them do need assistance. Fortunately, there are still people who know how to help them.

In this anthology, a dozen authors share their views on psychopomping in a variety of different Pagan and shamanic traditions, in terms of both personal experience and traditional ritual and myth. This book aims to educate the community about this vital practice, one that is still very much a necessary function. The word psychopomp comes from Greek roots meaning "soul conductor," and that's exactly what happens in this kind of work: the practitioner helps the spirit of the deceased find its way. The term deathwalking refers to the fact that shamans walk "between the worlds" and can help the spirits of the deceased journey onward as well. The actual practice goes by different names in different traditions, but the work is ultimately the same, and it's a loving, caring endeavor.

In modern society we tend to feel a bit mystified by death and spirits, perhaps even afraid of the whole kit-and-caboodle. Spirit workers (shamans and others who do this sort of work) have developed a relationship with the spirit world, journeying among the different realms, so to them it's familiar territory, as is death. We modern folk generally aren't close to death anymore; we die in hospitals and our bodies are whisked away to funeral homes, only to magically reappear, embalmed and made up, as if still alive. Even if someone else takes care of the nitty-gritty material details for us, though, death is still a part of our reality, albeit a more abstract one.

We're taught that death is off-putting and scary, but children are naturally curious about it and not generally afraid. Perhaps we adults could rekindle some of that gentle, loving curiosity and allow ourselves to learn about death and deathwalking, even if only in a small way. Some of the chapters in this collection include tales of closeness to death that the contributors have experienced in their own lives. Others share rituals, mythology, and traditions around the process of ensuring the spirit of the deceased gets to where it needs to go. It is our hope that these ideas and information will add meaning to your life and your spirituality, and perhaps lead you down new roads that you find fulfilling.

Some of you will simply enjoy the stories in this collection, learning about the various ways in which we're able to help the spirits of the dead move on. Others will want to learn more, perhaps get some training and join those who do this kind of work. Many of the chapters in this book end with recommendations of people and programs who offer instruction in psychopomp work. (Please note that since URLs can change, suggested resources are listed by program, course, or instructor name which you can search for online.) If you're interested, please investigate these resources and take your training seriously. This is one of those "don't try this at home" kinds of things; shamanic work of any sort requires the knowledge and safeguards that come with good education.

But especially, please accept our collection of information and anecdotes for what it ultimately is: a devotional of a sort, an offering to the spirits of all those who have gone before and all those who will come after. May they journey onward well.

Psychopomps and Psychopaths: Children in the role of psychopomp or soul conductor

Children are generally not afraid of death the way many adults are. Possibly because they have not been on the planet too long and often remember (even if vaguely, only in their dreams) where they were before they were born. My own middle son used to call this place Yellow Land (a land made of pure bright light) as a toddler. I once made a painting titled *The Before Life* (as we focus too much on the afterlife, but that is only one half of the coin!). In the summer of 2016 I made a short film about the young people in my shamanic program for children (The Time Travellers in London, UK) sharing their unique perspectives on death and dying. The title of this film is *Psychopaths and Psychopomps* because the children in my program have been known to confuse the two terms! If you type in my name and the title on YouTube, the film will appear.

Let me tell you a secret: Death and dying is one of our favorite sessions in the Wheel of the Year for the Time Travellers, yet I can barely drum up registrations for shamanic death and dying courses for adults. We live in a culture that is in denial about death. Death is feared and hidden from view, not embraced as the ally and the great teacher it really is.

When I was a child (growing up in the Netherlands in the seventies) I did a lot of work in other dimensions at night. Often the spirits would appear and say: please come and talk to this newly dead person. He or she is not really paying attention to us, but maybe they will listen to a young girl; you are closer to the world they have just left. So, I would go and spend time with the person concerned. I would explain that they were dead (they did not always realize this). I would show them around the spirit world and explain that there are compassionate beings (who may not look human) waiting to take them to the right destination in the other world. I would accompany them some of the way. Then I would hand them over to those beings and watch them "walk through a portal into the light." I would return to my bed in everyday reality and go to school the next morning. To me, this was as normal as brushing my teeth! I never really talked to my parents about this. I think my mother only found out about this forty years later when she painstakingly read my first book (*Natural Born Shamans: A Spiritual Toolkit for Life*) using an English-Dutch dictionary!

Today, I am a shamanic practitioner and I teach shamanism and sacred art internationally. Working with children has become one of my specialties. Over the years I have seen many children in private shamanic practice who are psychopomps. In this chapter I will share my experiences of this: what forms this can take, how it can affect family life, and what to do when such a child becomes overwhelmed or frightened.

Children as Psychopomps

I have come to believe that children are soul conductors or deathwalkers for many reasons. Some children are our future shamanic practitioners (or shamans) and this calling is already written into their energy signature.

Children come from the light, from outside time; sometimes they still radiate this divine light. Often they have not suffered the amount of soul loss some adults have, so energetically speaking they are very luminous, especially when they are loved greatly and well cared for. That can add power to their energy field.

Then again, children may also end up conducting psychopomp work for the opposite reason: trauma can "open children up" in the sense that they do not acquire healthy psychic boundaries in early life. This can leave children vulnerable to happenings in other realms, both in a good sense (sensing a loving grandparent watching over them and staying close) or in a negative sense (dissociating from pain and trauma by fleeing to other worlds and not being fully present in their own lives and bodies). This is a condition many people carry into their adult existence.

Other authors in this book have explained why the death process can be compromised, meaning a soul doesn't make a full transition away from the Earth realm. Such restless souls (for lack of a better word) are often found wandering between the worlds. For them, the bright energy signature of a "shaman child" is like a beacon. They are attracted to that light. They may even take it for the divine light they are seeking.

Some children (like the younger me) walk the worlds effortlessly, guided by spirit allies who have been their friends from well before birth. I was never afraid, even when presented with challenging scenarios. However, my brother went through a period in his late teens (he was seriously ill at the time) when ghosts and spirits were appearing in his bedroom. He'd often wake up because people were sitting on the edge of his bed trying to get his attention. For him, this was a frightening and unwanted experience. It stopped when he recovered and he certainly does not feel called to engage in psychopomp work today.

Effects on Family Life

When a child copes well and is rested enough to face the challenges of this world in the morning, there is little parents need to do other than (ideally!) becoming aware of this and being available if a child needs to talk or process. The problems start when children are flooded by nighttime occurrences or experiences they cannot handle. Those children may start avoiding sleep (by trying to stay awake at all costs and this, obviously, affects their health and ability to concentrate in school). They may become frightened and call out, getting their parents up several times a night. Those parents may not always understand what their children perceive, and saying "There is nothing in your room. Go back to sleep!" just is not adequate. Parents need to be aware that there may well be *unseen visitors* in a child's bedroom; those are real, even if you yourself cannot see or sense them!

In the worst case scenario (which, thankfully, is rare!) nighttime visitors may start wandering around the house trying to get everyone's attention, meaning strange things might occur (noises, lights flashing on and off, sudden changes in temperature) that unsettle (or frighten) the whole family.

If you find yourself in one of these scenarios, please contact a local shamanic practitioner and have them run a check on what is happening. They can provide a range of helpful services from visiting in person and opening portals (moving on those "visitors" by doing psychopomp work) to explaining to your child what is going on and taking measures to stop the problem. One way this is commonly achieved is by programming a quartz crystal to act as a *waiting room* between the worlds, meaning the uninvited callers move into that dedicated safe space and stay there awaiting assistance, and then emptying that crystal at regular intervals. Personally speaking, I receive such crystals in the post, clear them, re-program them and send them back. Some families have two: one crystal on active duty and one *change of guard,* so the child is free from disturbance at all times. Some families have several members with a talent for psychopomp work. In that case it is worth placing crystals in strategic places around the house. Again, a shamanic practitioner can offer advice on that.

A Word of Caution!

Please note:

- You must have the crystals emptied/cleared at regular intervals or they stop doing their job!
- Putting "any old crystal" in a child's bedroom will not

help – the crystal needs to be programmed specifically, monitored and cleared by a professional (and cannot have any other purpose).

• Younger siblings or family pets must be prevented from touching the crystal or walking around with it. Put it out of reach, perhaps high up!

I have invited parents to death and dying, and psychopomp workshops which I teach (the idea being that the parents could learn to empty the crystals themselves) but the uptake has not been great.

Children and Death

I was very pleased when Laura Perry (the coordinator of this anthology) invited me to write about children as soul conductors because it is an issue that can cause upheaval in family life (and serious stress between parents and children, if the issue is not understood). Following on from that, I want to say a few more things in general about children and death.

For children, the veil between the worlds is often thinner than for adults, meaning that it is not uncommon for children to see glimpses of (for instance) dead grandparents or angelic beings. I remember getting ready to take my own three children to school one morning and observed them all gazing at a point next to our front door saying: "Mum, there is a an angel standing by the door and he is much taller than you are!" It is of crucial importance not to ridicule or ignore such comments. (If you do, your children will shut down and not feel safe sharing such experiences in the future!). Parents need to make an immense effort to truly listen to their children without their own fears or prejudices getting in the way. Instead of saying "Don't be silly!" or "Such things do not exist!" try to say: "Please tell me more ... I cannot see it myself. Would you please draw for me what it looks like?" That way, the channels of communication stay open and a foundation is laid for a spiritual dialogue lasting throughout the teenage period even, and well into the young adolescent years.

If you have very young children (say under the age of five) you could also gently ask some questions (without leading them or freaking them out). If you are reading a book in which, for example, angels appear, just ask lightly: Have you ever seen an angel? After a grandparent or loved family friend dies (or even the family guinea pig), rather than being totally absorbed by your own grief (perhaps thinking that children are too young to be aware of such things) use those occasions to have important conversations with your children. Essentially such sad events are gifts and great learning opportunities.

Explore where your children think people and animals go after death. Try not to cut off all dialogues by saying, "They are in Heaven now!" (FULL STOP). Heaven is a highly simplified concept promoted by Christianity. I once invited my Time Travellers to make a journey through the other worlds and visit Heaven. They discovered many exciting and amazing locations but they did not find "the textbook realm of Heaven." (For more about all this, I invite you to read my book.)

One of the greatest gifts you can bestow on your (grand) children (assuming you have them) or any child (if you have access to children professionally speaking or in other ways) is to talk to them from a place of not fearing death. Death is hugely important in our cosmos because death feeds life. Without death everything would stagnate; there would be no renewal or rebirth. Help children become aware of the seasons and cycles of life. Host open-minded conversations about this so they see it is okay to talk about death and ask questions. A life lived without fear of death (or in denial of death) is the only way of living any human life to the full.

As one of my Time Travellers once summed up: *"We all get recycled!"*

How to Find a Practitioner or Teacher

If you need help with some of the issues described in this book, your first port of call is to contact your local shamanic practitioner. If you decide you wish to undertake training in this work, you need to find a death and dying course that includes psychopomp work, offered by an experienced shamanic teacher. A great starting point is Sandra Ingerman's website: Shamanism Teachers and Practitioners. It offers a global listing of practitioners (organized by location) as well as many courses in shamanism and related subjects offered by shamanic teachers who have trained with Sandra herself. Some other good resources are The Society for Shamanic Practice, Shaman Links, and the Foundation of Shamanic Studies. These offer listings of shamanic practitioners and teachers who can help you.

Imelda Almqvist's book *Natural Born Shamans: A Spiritual Toolkit for Life (Using shamanism creatively with young people of all ages)* was published by Moon Books on 26 August 2016. She is based in London, UK and teaches shamanism and sacred art internationally. You can find her online at shaman-healer-painter.co.uk

Midwife to the Dying: The Post-Tribal Shaman's Role

Immortality is composed of equal portions of life and death.
— Grandfather

All of us will die. This is certain. For some it will be sudden and unexpected, but for most of us, it will be a gradual process, coming at the end of a long life. Yet, in spite of its universal nature, death is perhaps the most taboo subject in our Western culture. So much so that many doctors still hesitate to let their patients know when they have a terminal diagnosis. Even family members, coming to say their last goodbyes, often avoid talking about why they are there, out of fear of the discomfort that arises when addressing the specter of death – discomfort that is more on the part of those who will survive than on that of the dying. This leaves the person going through the process of departing life without real support or connection through this difficult transition. One of the important roles of the shaman in our culture is to provide this support and to help the client develop the connections necessary to allow death to be a natural and peaceful passing from one state to another.

In traditional tribal culture, as a person nears the end of their natural lifespan, they begin to pay more attention to the spiritual – to those parts that will remain after their bodies are gone. They become closer to their ancestors and begin to loosen their hold on the physical world. But even for those who die unexpectedly or die of disease while still young, there is the expectation and awareness of a larger existence than what is experienced in this life. There is an understanding that there is more to them than their individual identities, bodies, and minds. In most of these cultures, the soul is seen as having different parts: One that comes from the ancestors; one that comes from the stars; one that is born with and dies with the physical body. There is a sense that, while part of us dies with the body, part of us continues as well. When you consider that in our modern Western culture it is the physical and mental elements of ourselves that we are most focused on, giving little to no attention to the spiritual aspects of self, it is unsurprising that we would feel fearful when looking at the end of life.

Most in our culture view the process of death as something primarily dealt with by the living. We grieve for the loss of those who have died, and reshape our lives around those losses. But from the shaman's point of view, those who have already died are integral to the process as well. Since we regularly interact with the ancestors through our work, we do not share the idea that the world is populated only by the living. It is our ability to Journey into the underworld – the place of the Dead – that allows us to be of service to those who are dying, even after death. As shamans, we Journey into the other worlds regularly, returning safely with healing and information for our clients.

Essentially, three types of shamanism are practiced today. Indigenous traditions, maintained and practiced by existing tribal peoples also include practitioners who have been adopted into these cultures, or reconstructionists, who base their practices on what is known, believed, or fantasized about a particular culture's shamanic practices. Core shamanic practitioners use what they see as universal practices of the indigenous people. Finally, there are those in the modern Western world who have developed their practice based on their connection with and initiation by the spirits. Post-Tribal Shamanism falls into this latter category. The teachings I pass on to others are those I received from my own spirit ally, Grandfather. In most cases, these teachings have much in common with those of other shamanic traditions.

The definition of shamanism we use in Post-Tribal Shamanism is much the same as in other traditions. A shaman is someone who goes into a trance state at will, to communicate with and interact with spirits, in order to bring about changes and retrieve information in service to others.

In Post-Tribal Shamanism, we understand the human soul as having multiple components. The Ancestral Soul includes all of a person's bloodline and is communal in nature. The Celestial Soul has lived many prior lifetimes and will go on to other lifetimes after we die. The Egoic Soul is our thinking, self-identified part. Grandfather teaches that at death, the ancestral soul and celestial soul generally leave the body, while the egoic soul tends to stay with the physical remains until it gradually dissolves into the natural surroundings. For most of us, there are representatives of our ancestors awaiting us as our souls emerge from the body at death. They are usually people we knew while they were alive and with whom we have a strong, loving connection. They then serve as guides as we travel into the lower world. This journey, which the Tibetans refer to as the bardo, affords us an opportunity to address unresolved issues from our recently completed lifetime.

Much of what we can do with a client depends on where they are in their process when we are first consulted and on their attitudes toward death. If we have months to work with the person, we may help them to develop an awareness of the part of themselves that will continue after death, thus easing much of the fear. We can teach them how to Journey into the lower world, where they can communicate directly with their ancestors and reassure themselves of what awaits them. Given time, we can even teach them practices that allow them to take their egoic soul along with the other soul parts after death, ensuring that they will be able to maintain the continuity of their consciousness, even as their identity transforms. This also gives us the opportunity to assure them that the ancestors are aware of the impending demise and that someone will be present to welcome the dying person.

In many cases, we are not called on until the person is already on their deathbed, and there is only time to Journey to assure that there are ancestors who can assist them. This is generally not a problem, but there are situations where the ancestral soul has become so depleted or disconnected that the person's ancestors never knew that they were there. This can be due to a combination of systemic trauma, drug addiction, adoption, and soul-level wounding.

In situations where there is no connection with the ancestors, the shaman takes their place at the side of the dying person, welcoming them into the afterlife as they emerge into soul. There is often a point in the dying process, even if the client is no longer conscious, where they seem to give up the fight and let go of any remaining life force. This energy floods out into the room, even making those who are there feel intoxicated or euphoric. After this, it is not long before the final breath. If I am at the bedside, this is when I will move into shamanic body and prepare myself for their soul to rise out of the body.

It would be a mistake to think that something as mysterious as mortality can be addressed with a simple "how to" guide. The experience is always different, and yet there are underlying commonalities that allow us to navigate safely.

I was introduced to "Sam" by his rabbi. As we talked, Sam told me matter-of-factly that he had a terminal diagnosis from brain cancer. He felt he had lived a good life. His wife had died years before and his children were both grown. He seemed to accept his fate. He made it clear that he did not believe in God and had no expectation of an afterlife, but that he was experiencing anxiety around what would happen, and was hoping that I would be able to help him with that.

My first priority was to guide Sam into Soul Awareness – a meditative state in which the ego takes refuge in the non-dual awareness of the soul. Once he was able to rest in this luminous field of awareness, his anxiety diminished and he seemed much more at ease.

As we wrapped up our third session, I was about to suggest to Sam that he had the skill to meditate and keep his anxiety in check now, so I didn't see any reason to schedule another session. He interrupted me by asking me, "Do you believe there is something after death?"

I told him, "Sam. I used to get confused, because sometimes I did believe in an afterlife, and sometimes I didn't. When I started working with Grandfather, my spirit ally and mentor, he taught me that there are parts of us that die with the body, while other parts go on into the afterlife. So, in a way, both answers are correct. Part of us will not experience anything after the death of our bodies, but part of us will."

After some thought, Sam decided to continue working with me. He was able to learn how to move into his shamanic body and to Journey into the Underworld where he reconnected with the spirits of his wife and parents. This impacted him powerfully, allowing him to release most of the anxiety and be at peace for the last few weeks of his life.

I wasn't able to be at his bedside when Sam passed. But I Journeyed there and was able to watch as his wife and parents met him and he began his Journey into the afterlife. He had died at home and I was able to visit shortly afterwards. I used a bottle of saltwater to gather his remaining egoic soul from around his body, rather like sopping up water with a sponge. His family had asked me to speak at his memorial and to release his spirit by an old oak tree that had been one of his favorite places. I poured the saltwater over the roots of the tree and wished him well.

Sam was an easy case. Many are not. "Nadine" was dying of throat cancer, but she was determined not to go. She told me that the chemo had worked and that she was free of cancer, but that she was seeing me because she needed to get herself back together. It was pretty clear to me that she was not doing well and that the cancer was still present and spreading. I asked her if she had been given a prognosis by her doctor and she told me they said she was as "fit as a fiddle." I'm not sure if they were lying to her or if she was lying to me, but it was clearly not true.

As she continued to deteriorate over the next few months, I tried to address with her the process of dying several times but she was never interested. Even when she went into hospice, she was determined that she was going to "beat this."

Nadine requested a house call shortly before she died. I asked how her relationship was with her parents. They had died many years before, and she didn't feel any particular connection with them. Then she told me, "But of course, they're not really my parents. I was adopted." I asked her if she had ever found her biological parents, but she said she had never been interested. I Journeyed for her, in search of her ancestors, and finally was able to track them down. They had no sense of connection with her, and it was difficult for me to even get their attention, but at least I knew where she needed to go. I was hoping to teach her how to Journey and bring her into the Underworld to meet her ancestors, but it turned out we didn't have time. She died a few days later. Her companion called to tell me that she was passing and I arrived in time to watch her take her last breath.

I moved into shamanic body and stood beside her bed. After a couple of minutes her soul seemed to drift out of her body, as if it had just come loose. She was unresponsive, but I managed to draw her through the doorway into Lodge and then we Journeyed down the World Tree and into the Underworld. At times she seemed to shudder and shake spasming with strong emotion or struggling to escape something. I kept her contained and waited until she could continue. When we arrived at the place of her ancestors, I was worried. I didn't want to leave her here without any connection. As I drew her into the space, the ancestors that were there backed away and seemed disinterested. Then another ancestor arrived from deeper in the space. She felt to me like a warm, loving grandmother. She took Nadine into her embrace and rocked her, and I knew that it was okay for me to leave.

We can never know what the right thing to do will be, but one awareness guides all of our actions: that dying is a natural process, which is part of a greater whole. Because of this, we do as little as possible in order to allow this process to proceed with ease and acceptance. When the individual feels themselves slipping into this flow, fear tends to fall away, allowing a peaceful transition.

Kenn Day is a professional shaman who lives and works in Cincinnati, Ohio in the US, with his beloved wife and daughter. He has published two books on shamanism through Moon Books: *Dance of Stones: A Shamanic Road Trip* and *Post-Tribal Shamanism: A New Look at the Old Ways.* He passes on Grandfather's teachings in a series of workshops offered internationally. You can find more about Kenn online at shamanstouch.com

Deathwalking with the Living: A shamanic healer's perspective

As a shamanic healer I need to be prepared for anything when I begin a healing session. Each and every client is different and comes with all that they have accumulated moving through their lives. In principle, a shamanic healing is likely to incorporate some of the following: energy field alignment or balancing, clearing or releasing of unwanted energy, often described as entity removal, power retrieval and soul retrieval, what actually happens during each session and how I work is always unique to the client I am working with. Very rarely I may come across a need to perform an energy or entity removal where the misplaced energy is that of a soul that has passed. This is extremely rare and is not the same thing as possession where someone is completely taken over by another entity, even rarer still and something I have never experienced. The type of thing I am talking about is where for some reason, instead of passing over, the soul of the departed being attaches itself to the energy of another person.

As I said, this does not happen often and in no way does every occurrence of misplaced energy turn out to be a lost soul who needs to be shown how to pass into the light. In my experience from when I have encountered a deceased soul, the soul has attached for completely different reasons and has also needed a different form of assistance in order to leave their host.

Whilst I am obviously not able to share the exact healing journey of individual clients, the following two examples are based upon actual healing sessions and describe, from my perspective, ways that the soul of someone who has passed can be helped to move on from the client to a more appropriate place. Moving the energy, releasing it and helping it move on can be very beneficial for both parties.

Example 1

Part of my practice is always to allow time for the client to talk. I find this helps me to connect with them and also to begin to assess them. On this occasion I had a client who described a feeling of having a "twin" attached to them, starting at their head and continuing down their side.

While they were talking, I had been gazing with a soft gaze so that I could view their energy field. The energy they spoke of was clearly visible to me as a pink, red, and orange cloud that extended down their right side. Connecting with it, I had the sense of a female energy. It didn't feel aggressive in any way, in fact quite the opposite.

When carrying out a shamanic healing, I always get the client to lie on my treatment table. I usually begin by checking the energy body and energy flow. I have several ways of doing this but on this occasion I used sage. My client's body repelled the sage completely, so I decided to begin with a sage clearing of the whole energy field. I worked with sage, brushing the smoke with a large condor feather, over her body, through her energy field, focusing on the right side, all the time holding the intention to clear the energy field and begin the process of detachment. I sat with one of my hands on the right-hand side of her head and the other on her knee, and shifted into light trance.

Almost straight away I could see the entity behind the attached energy. It was a female in her early twenties, long red hair tied back and dressed in a pink and orange dress. She gave me her name and said that she meant no harm. She told me that she had been lost, had found my client and that she loved and wanted to help her. With her was a young black and white cat, very playful and active. I explained to her that she was in fact distressing my client and that she was in fact causing her harm.

Whilst we were talking I became aware of a light that started somewhere behind me as a tiny pin prick, grew, moved around my right-hand side and in front of me into the entity's view. As it did I asked if she was willing to leave if I helped her find her way and she whispered "thank you."

At this point the light was quite large and very bright. Out of it stepped a young male dressed in Elizabethan clothes: a doublet and hose. He held out his hand, spoke her name and the entity moved towards him and took hold of his hand. She waved goodbye, said "thank you" again and moved off into the light. The cat, all this time, had been running back and forth between my client's right-hand side and the light. Before I could do anything, a pure black adult cat walked out of the light, spoke to the young cat which ran behind her into the light. The light, then, immediately vanished.

I sat and ran energy into the space left in my client's energy field so that no vacuum remained. I picked up my rattle and a piece of black tourmaline which I placed on the chair beside me. Holding the intention to clear any residual imbalance of energy, I worked with the rattle, collecting any sticky or misplaced energy and directed it into the stone which accepted it willingly. To complete the session, I drummed over my client, allowing the drum to find the vibration it needed to complete the healing.

Example 2

My client arrived in quite a distressed state, speaking of how they were constantly tired, drained and emotional, that they felt stuck and unable to do what they wanted to. They explained that they felt there was "something" that was stopping them, of how they believed that in the womb they had been one of a twin but the twin had not survived and they felt that it was the twin that was what holding them back in their life, not letting them move on.

Viewing their energy, I could see what I believed to be the location of the problem, although their energy was generally bright, over the heart and down the front of their abdomen was quite murky and stagnant. I confirmed this by using an egg, rolling it over the client's body and breaking it into a glass. By watching the formation of the egg white around the yolk I was able to interpret this as misplaced energy, most likely in the form of the twin soul that needed to be removed and helped to pass into the light.

Whilst discussing the ways in which I could help release the passed soul of the "twin," the client was concerned about losing the connection with the sibling. This was a hugely emotional experience as it was a personal attachment formed before birth and, so, on the understanding that the choice would ultimately be that of the passed soul's, I offered the possibility of rehoming the soul in a vessel so that it could be released from my client's energy but still kept close. A stone was chosen by my client who spoke of a special place in the garden where it could be placed, if it were the right thing for the soul.

Sitting and connecting with the entity, I found myself talking with a male who explained that he was my client's twin. The soul told me that he wished to stay where he was as he wanted to remain close to his twin forever; that he did not wish to leave. Thus we entered a long period of negotiation as to the soul's options and the reasons why he needed to let go and move on. The options were basically to move to the light and continue his journey or to be rehomed in the vessel so that he could still be nearby.

During negotiations with any entity, passed soul or not, it is usual to have to present the alternatives as well as to explain, often at length, why their staying where they are is not a good idea. This time was no different. With most lost souls there is no desire to hurt the host and by explaining the damage they are doing to the host, even when they wish to stay, it is usually possible to persuade them otherwise. In this instance I explained that while his twin loved him and did not want to lose him, he was, in fact, being harmed. I explained all that my client had shared with me and asked my client if he too would like to talk with his "twin." This he did despite it, obviously, being emotionally difficult for him.

During this discussion, I became aware of a light opening in front of me and a woman walked through. She introduced herself as the mother of the twins and asked if she might intercede. She explained to the passed soul that it was time to go and asked him to take her hand and go with her. Again this was refused. She then reiterated that it was time to leave and that the vessel of the stone was the only other way. This time he agreed to move into the stone, the woman stepped back and the light vanished.

I placed the stone in my client's hand with my hand over the top of both and together we held the stone over the abdominal area where the soul had been residing. My client explained where the stone was to be placed and how he loved the soul. At this, the passed soul left the body and went into the stone.

While my client held his "twin" close, I continued with the session, clearing anything remaining and then ensured that no vacuum was left behind now that the energy of the passed soul had moved on.

Yvonne Ryves was born and lived in England for most of her life but it was a move to Ireland that drew her to her present path as a Shamanic Healer, Reiki Master, Chios Energy Master/ Teacher and Past Life Regression Therapist. In addition, she runs workshops and courses on a variety of aspects of energy healing and shamanic work including Reiki, Chios, Munay-Ki, Shamanic Journeying, Pendulum Dowsing and self-development. Yvonne also holds a Certificate in Counseling, a Teaching Certificate, a BA and MSc in Education and is currently training as an Ovate with the Order of Bards, Ovates and Druids (OBOD). Yvonne is the author of *Shaman Pathways – Web of Life: Guidance for Your Life Journey* and is a contributor to the anthology *Pagan Planet: Being, Believing and Belonging in the 21st Century*. You can find her online at yvonneryves.com

Reality, Spirit, and Death

In the British old ways, we know that death is part of life; they're two sides of one coin.

Amongst animals and plants, the old, the weak and the young are often, indeed, food for others; plants are food for animals, birds, fish and insects as well as humans; we all feed on each other. This is not horrible; it's the *wholeness* of Lovelock's Gaia. Mother Earth feeds and nourishes all her creatures, and nothing, no animal or plant wishes to live forever.

Humans are the only species that broods on, and fears, old age and death. All our elder brethren, all the non-human life of Earth, grows old and dies with relative grace. For the past nearly seventy years cats have shared my life; come the end, they will often go off to find a peaceful place to quietly slip away and die. I've been privileged to be with three of them as their spirits sliped out of their Earth-shell. I work as a psychopomp so I've also watched with many human-friends while they do the same thing. I utterly disagree with Dylan Thomas' words, "*Do not go gentle into that good night, Old age should burn and rave at close of day; Rage, rage against the dying of the light.*" To me, this is the grasping, childish attitude of the personal-self that has no concept of reality, let alone any connection with the divine.

I remember on Orkney, watching oyster catchers land softly on the seaweed-covered rocks, flutter their wings, pipe their evensong to each other as they came down to the rock pools to hunt and fish. A curlew bubbled and trilled too, disturbed from her hunting for a moment by the black-and-white evening-comers, but soon she was quiet again, walking the rocks, hunting her food. The waves boomed, thundered and then hissed away as they slithered back into the ocean, only to come again a moment later. Dancing waves and rocks, a place of meetings and partings, every moment made anew, then gone, only to come again, but differently. Death and rebirth, everything changing, only so does everything remain. I was overawed by what the natural world showed me about death.

I learned my craft from my family and the wise folk, both women and men, of the village. Our next door neighbor was a healer and the village midwife who also performed the laying out of the dead. She was a transition lady, doorkeeper and threshold holder of both the coming into and the going out of life. We youngsters would be detailed to help her with both births and deaths so we got to know what babies and old, dead bodies looked like, where they came from and went to, and not to be afraid of them, nor of the process of death.

We learned-by-doing that birth and death are two sides of the same coin, that coming into this world is leaving otherworld and vice versa. Back in the 1950s, home-births were the norm; you only went to hospital if it looked dangerous. The doctor would come round to help if necessary but it was mostly all down to the midwife ... and her assistants, us village children. We learned how to greet the new young humans into their incarnation.

It was similar with death, we learned how to say farewell to those who died. Again, in the village, when a person died, the doctor would come and pronounce death, sign the certificate and then the midwife took over. Funeral parlors were expensive; people only used them when they couldn't do the necessary things for themselves. And anyway, it's much nicer if a friend looks after your body when you've passed over and have no more use for it, home composting.

The rituals were simple but profound. The first thing was the washings, first with water then with smoke. One of the older girls prepared the water; something I did after my first-blood of puberty. We used the elder tree. First the leaves were steeped overnight in water from the village's sacred well which my aunt owned and was guardian to; its story goes way back four thousand years. She, and my gardening-uncle, lived in the well-cottage with the well itself set in the wall between our garden and theirs, there was a pump then, so you could draw the water but that's all gone now.

Next day, we would boil up elderberries in the water the leaves had steeped in. If fresh berries weren't available (as was often the case) we used elder vinegar made over the previous autumn. Either way, the washing-water came up a beautiful wine-color.

While we youngsters washed the corpse in the elder-water, the midwife prepared the smoke-wash. She would choose which herbs to use depending on the person and the season, then we children would be sent out to find them, many of our parents grew them in the garden but some came from the wild hedges.

The washings are all about conversing with the spirit that had recently inhabited the body. You spend the time of the washings making sure all is as it should be, and the spirit content, before giving the body back to the Earth. Relatives would do this with us too, chatting with the spirit until it was ready to go.

After the water and air washings, the corpse would be returned to Mother Earth through burial or cremation, earth or fire. But there was always a celebratory fire at the wake even if the person had been buried, and there would always be ritual earth sprinkled if it was a cremation – always the four elements. This burial or cremation happened after the spirit had fully left the body, usually after three days. Back in the 1950s the bodies were kept at home for that time, often on the dining room table, if there was a dining room, in the coffin. Friends, neighbors, and relations would come to pay their respects.

The final celebration, the wake, happened after the burial or cremation, and often included singing – we called it Enchanting – and people would drum using stones or woodblocks as well as drums, sounding hawk bells, and I've seen folk knocking horse brasses together, too. The wakes were communal affairs organized by everyone and for everyone, making and bringing food and drink, sharing the celebration of someone we'd all known.

Sometimes there would be problems in the preparation of the spirit and the body. One time when I was about sixteen, we were helping this man who had been killed in a fight to cross over. It was quite an effort because it was actually he who had started the fight, and had been killed by his friend. He needed to make his peace with his friend who was still alive but badly injured in hospital. It took some organizing and I was the one chosen to do the work, to visit the hospital and sit with the injured man, as I'd known both of them. I sat beside him and connected myself to the group by the corpse, I then worked between the two, transmitting what the living man wanted and telling him what his dead friend said. It worked. The dead man was unhappy and very sorry, while the injured man was very angry; it took a lot of talking before he would absolve and release his dead friend. When you do this sort of thing it just doesn't allow you to have the usual misconceptions about death.

I dropped out of the circle, the group who did the death rituals, when I left home to go to university.

The first death I was fully part of was right back in 1952 when I was three years old, my own mother's death and wake. There was no way Dad would let me be shut out of it. I watched the washings happen, the old folk (old in spirit though not always in years) involved me in it, made me feel part of it and, in consequence, I never felt abandoned. Gradually, from those initial baby-steps, I was able to hang more and more knowing onto the memories and make real sense of them, really understand death.

Mum was laid out in her coffin on the dining room table, friends came to say goodbye. The night before the burial, Dad and a few friends all sat around singing her off and I was there, part of it. Next day, we took her up to the churchyard to be buried, it was on top of a cliff looking out over the Bristol Channel; Dad said she'd enjoy the view. I remember holding his hand as we stood beside the grave, asking, "Mummy's not in the box is she? Where's she gone?" Dad replied, "No lovey, only her body is in the box. She's gone home to otherworld where she'll get better." Mum died of cervical cancer in 1952 when there was very little known and not much anyone could do about it. I never forgot Dad's words.

Forty years later he followed her.

I'd not been able to be there to sit-with Dad as he passed over but Vera, my stepmother, was. She told me about it when I came down for the burial. She'd sat beside him on the bed, held his hand, watched his connection with his body gradually thinning until finally, with a deep heaving breath, he let go. Then the cord sparkled and shimmered, got brighter and brighter and more and more tenuous until it was just a very bright light disappearing incredibly fast into a velvet blackness. Bright darkness, she called it.

The rituals for Dad – and Vera fifteen months later – were much shorter and all the body washing was gone as the bodies were given over to the undertakers. I found that strange and disconnected, but I was able to do the sit-with rituals with them both, and that was good. Then, after the burials, the wakes; both Dad's and Vera's wakes were lovely, Dad's at our cottage and Vera's in the village hall. They were still communal celebrations, everyone brought food and drink, contributed, it was ours, our celebration, belonging to the folk who'd known Dad and Vera, in the place they lived and loved.

Vera loved Dad very much so she didn't want to stay after he'd gone. She hung on for fifteen months, then had a series of strokes culminating in a neighbor finding her on the kitchen floor in a coma, with our old dog sat beside, watching over her. They rushed her to hospital and phoned me. Again, I wasn't able to be there with her but one of her best friends was.

The doctor kept phoning to tell me what was happening. She'd gone in with a heart attack, within hours they found she had lung cancer – Dad smoked like a chimney – soon they found she had septicemia, next her liver gave up, then her kidneys failed. I asked why they couldn't just let her go as she wanted. The doctor said it was because Vera was so young, only seventy-two, so they were legally bound to try to prolong her life.

That was horrible to me. I knew, absolutely, that Vera was doing her damndest to die despite what the doctors were doing. I phoned a bunch of friends – by "accident" there were thirteen of us – from all over the world and asked everyone to be there, in spirit, at 5pm GMT, and for us all to send energy to Vera so she could do with it what she willed. We did that thing. At 5.20pm the doctor phoned to say Vera had passed over, very quietly and peacefully. At last I was able to cry, and with joy because Vera had her wish at last.

The group compared notes later; we'd all had similar pictures in our mind's eye, Vera in the hospital bed with her friend sat beside her, holding her hand. Then intense light with a hand reaching out, taking Vera's hand and leading her away. At the wake, a few days later, Vera's friend took me aside, told me what had happened. She'd seen the light and the hand too, and Vera's cord had brightened then rushed away into the light and she was gone.

"And what were you up to, then," she asked me, "I weren't alone there with her, there were a whole pack with you." I smiled back, "Of course," I said. "You didn't think I'd forsake her did you?" We chuckled and went off to get another cuppa and rejoin everyone in the celebrating of Vera's life.

Elen Sentier writes mystery-romance novels. She has been writing all her life and professionally since 1999. She is a wilderness woman, born on Dartmoor, grew up on the edge of Exmoor, and comes from a long line of British cunning folk, so, she also writes about and teaches British native shamanism. She now lives with her husband, cats, and a host of wildlife in the wild Welsh Marches of Britain. She is the author of several *Shaman Pathways* books including *The Celtic Chakras*, *Elen of the Ways*, *Following the Deer Trods*, and *Trees of the Goddess*. She has also written *Gardening with the Moon and Stars* and *Pagan Portals – Merlin: Once and Future Wizard*. You can find her online at elensentier.co.uk

Deathwalking with Reluctant Spirits

In working with souls who have not crossed from this world to the next, deathwalkers will meet individuals who resist leaving this world. Spirits residing on this side of the veil are convinced they should remain earthbound. The skilled deathwalker becomes a between-the-worlds counselor to listen without judgment. We suggest ways for the spirits to release themselves from their ties. We reason with them and point out the illogic of staying in place. We facilitate their healing with spiritual first aid. Our efforts are not appreciated. The spirits argue or fight back. Transitioning spirits with large soul wounds take intervention from other spirits, some from the otherside, so we never work in isolation. Some of the stories are heartbreaking. Some are frightening. Still others are simply frustrating. Our task is to help the lost find a way to put their issues to rest and initiate their journey into the Light. When we have their agreement, we take them through ordinary reality to the Light where they are greeted by loved ones. Then we are careful to turn and walk away. It is not our time.

What ties people to this world? Fear of retribution on the other side from their victims. Anger against souls who have abused them in this life and preceded them in death. Fear of judgment from an angry God. Fear of purgatory. Grief at leaving their loved ones behind. Responsibility for unfinished business. Their family at loose ends after a sudden death. Horror at one's own suicide. Anger at a God who allowed a horrible death/ execution. Mental illness that infects the soul. A belief that death ends our consciousness and there is nothing to transition to. Ties to a particular geography, energy vortex or being stuck in an energy glob that draws people in to refuel its powerful emotion and create itself as an entity. Rejection of the deathwalker. Heartaches we can only guess.

Discovering what ties the soul to our dimension would defeat me entirely if I were not traveling with my animal allies or spirit guides who direct my journey. Shamanic healing work requires consultation with my guides and those who shelter the client to assure the success of the venture. If in an open discussion the guides express doubt or reject the healing intervention, I rethink the entire working. If no middle ground can be reached with them, I decline the opportunity, leaving it for another time or another person. That is rare. Usually we can create a positive way forward. The advantages the guides bring include greater creativity. I might not think of the right questions or miss hints about barriers to the transition through death into the life of Light. Disincarnate souls are no more forthcoming than people with bodies when asked about personal pain. By traveling with my guides and those of the lost soul, we can hear what is unspoken and understand the subtext.

The participation of guides and allies also strengthens my personal protection. Spirits can refuse assistance and stalk a well-meaning helper. Some spirits can levitate and throw objects, so physical injury is possible. They can attach to a particularly bright light. Attachment of that nature is not healthy. I make sure I am carrying appropriate crystals and stones, wearing a medicine bag or ring, and am deeply grounded with my belly chakra closed. My throat chakra is guarded and sealed in the back behind my neck. My heart is filled with higher consciousness compassion. Soul level interventions require love and power in combination and multiplied by the guides. Without that, deathwalking is a fool's journey.

There are then at least two journeys in deathwalking. One assesses the task and identifies the spirit helpers. We set up the boundaries and protections. The second journey contacts the soul and initiates the journey into the Light. A difficult transition could involve additional journeys when I might return with more information, gifts or offerings. I should say in all these journeys

I have a close friend or shamanic partner drum for me. That individual is skilled enough to extend Earth or celestial energy to me as I go. This also enhances my protection as I engage a soul who is stuck out of time and place. In the second journey, I ask my guides to take me to the correct location where we might find the soul. I experience a flying journey through the middle world. Usually I see known landmarks. Sometimes one of my allies acts as a tour guide, pointing out interesting features on the way. In a recent journey I flew over the African Rift Valley up into the Middle East. After I registered my surprise, I was joined by several Earth Mother Spirits who circled around the nation of Syria and spiraled in to Aleppo. I couldn't have been more astonished. I expected to work with hurricane victims in the US.

When we have set foot on the ground, I take inventory of the scene and ask questions. Is the soul near? Is there any danger here from mortals? From other spirits? What do I need to look for? The last thing I wanted was to be caught in a fire fight or a second tap in a war zone.

We then proceed through the middle world reality seeking the lost soul. There may be more than one. Which one am I to work with? Are there several who would move together to the Light? In the journey to Aleppo, I was brought first to a single boy sitting with his dead mother's body. She had crossed. He had seen his living father and brothers leave him behind as they rode away in the back of a truck. He didn't know what to do so he returned to his mother's body and that of his dog, not realizing he was dead, too. He insisted on waiting. One of my guides whistled and the dog ran back to urge his boy home. The boy was ready to follow the pup. I was irrelevant but I went along to the passageway, to the Light. When we reached the portal, it was filled with debris. My guides readily moved trees, rubble, chunks of masonry that would have taken more physical strength than I had. When the portal was cleared, the dog ran through to the boy's mother who waited at the gate. Then his father and brothers joined them from within the Light. They had drowned in the Mediterranean seeking asylum. Their reunion was sweet and heartbreaking at the same time. I would have been unaware of the details had I not been closely connected to the guides for that journey.

I expected that was enough for one journey but the guides took me to a bombed-out school with 16 school boys still sitting in rows waiting for someone to direct them. As I convinced them to follow me, not easy because I was an infidel woman, one of my guides urged me to ask about their sisters. It turns out the girls were together in one house. The boy who lived there readily took me to them even though his peers were not convinced we should. The cultural divide was deep. Do girls have souls? Can an American woman be trusted? Is this a trick of Satan? (Evangelical Christians have asked the same questions.) What I did was to cover my hair and ask them if they loved their sisters. Did they play together when they were little? Would they want them to escape this dark, horrible war? Love is the key to any of these barriers. The boys wanted to leave and take the girls with them if only because their city was destroyed. They needed permission to leave and I gave it to them.

Meanwhile, I proceeded through Aleppo with the 16 boys and 9 girls, back past the school on the way to the portal. We were stopped by the boys' Imam who was convinced I was kidnapping them. He knew he was dead but feared losing the children's souls to Satan (me). We had a debate of wits while the children stood on one leg and then the other, waiting for the adults to stop arguing. I finally convinced him by agreeing he had every reason to distrust me, but the fact remained, I knew where the portal was and he did not. He couldn't let that get by him, so we all went together. When the children saw the opening they ran through it, deaf to the Imam's warnings. He still thought it was a trick and wouldn't go. Finally, I asked what it would take for him to believe he could go into the Light himself. He demanded an escort of the archangels. Quickly four of my guides shape shifted into the required form. With wings and golden staves they escorted him through the gate into the Light, assuring me they would sort it all out later. A soul gets what is expected or required when they move into the Light. Sometimes it plays to their personal mythology. That's acceptable. My journey was done. Later, I recognized the spirits had taken me to a soul that was exactly my stumbling block, one who would challenge every bias in me. I did the work anyway. I saw him from the inside out and loved him.

Not all resistant souls are as hostile as the Imam. Some are stubborn. I encountered one while vacationing in Cornwall who was not so easily convinced. He had been the spiritual chief of a settlement thousands of years ago and knew all the techniques. He could see his guides and mine. He knew he was dead. He refused to cross because his sister had murdered him and her husband, the village leader. She was a powerful sorcerer in her own right who believed he had murdered their parents with poisons. He thought she might be right, that his medicines were prepared incorrectly or he had misidentified the plants. He was paralyzed with guilt so he haunted the mound where he was buried and the area where he had lived. I found him because both areas made me ill. When I journeyed to discover why, there he was, gruff and distrustful.

I learned his story gradually in ordinary consciousness. I roused from a dream, went to the living room of our flat and sat the night with him, hearing his story and finding a thread of something new from the twenty-first century to tell him. *Medical errors.* Doctors make medical errors. Even a proven prescription can kill some people because of allergic reactions. The law does not call that murder. *The inability to heal everyone.* Sometimes death is the healing. *Souls learn in-between lives.* His sister had moved on to new lessons and he had not. Several hours later we both gave up. He wanted to walk the seacoast again from his grave to his house. I fell asleep. When I woke the next morning and called, he was gone. He knew the way across. He was a deathwalker. He had said I should call him Joseph. I went looking for a translation of that name typical of the period and found none. Instead I learned Joseph means wizard.

On these occasions, as in other journeys, I gave thanks to these souls that taught me more about the human condition. I thanked my guides with commitment to the work. I take respite leave from what is difficult magic, but I always come back. I also keep an open inventory of my own soul as an offering to the guides. Where am I stubborn, prejudiced, blocked and judgmental? Our world's political climate makes that clearer than it ever has been. I pour love on those places in my heart and keep dissolving the chunks of grief and bitterness so I can grow into a better channel. No different than the next soul, I pay my own journey forward by walking others to their Light beings because I'm okay and so are they.

I am available for shamanic healing, soul retrieval and deathwalking and will take an occasional apprentice who is committed to the practice at an intermediate or advanced level. I also work with Bekki Shiningbearheart and Soft Moon Rising who offer the same services and more, including basic instruction in shamanic journeying. All three of us can be contacted through the Web PATH Center website or through our individual Facebook pages.

Dorothy Abrams is a witch and shamanic practitioner at the Web PATH Center in Lyons, NY, a spiritual center she co-founded in 1993. She is trained in core shamanism by graduates of Michael Harner's Foundation for Shamanic Studies and has led shamanic trance circles for 20 years. She teaches basic shamanic practice, shamanic healing and intervention at the Web PATH Center. She recently led the Web's Shamanic Intensive: Gaia Consciousness which included deathwalking in conjunction with recent natural disasters and the war dead. Dorothy is the author of *Identity and the Quartered Circle: Studies in Applied Wicca*. She is also the scribe and editor of the community book *Sacred Sex and Magick* by the Web PATH Center and has contributed to several other Moon Books anthologies including *Paganism 101, Naming the Goddess,* and *The Goddess in America*. Dorothy writes from her home in the New York lake district where she lives with her husband Eric Reynolds and their many rescued cats. Dorothy can be reached through her Facebook page: facebook.com/Dorothy-L-Abrams-Writers-Page or through the Web PATH's Facebook pages searchable as Web PATHCenter, Sacred Sex and Magick, and WebPATH Center Shamanism.

Hindu Last Rites

Death is a sensitive subject for most of us. Even if we believe in reincarnation, there is something final about a death that feels like it has closed the door to having a connection again to a person who has died. It signifies the end of a chapter that can never be reopened. Of course, it is the end of the current life of the body we inhabit. There is a lot about death that remains unknown. On a spiritual level, death offers us insight into understanding our greater purpose. In Hinduism, the first 13 days after death are essential and generally observed through rituals and prayers. As a child, I was aware that rituals and final rites were crucial to help not only the mourning process but also for the soul to move on. We believe that the souls are circling the body and the family around those first few days. Our thoughts and feelings are communicated at that juncture.

While we do not have shamanic deathwalking practices in traditional Hinduism per se, we do acknowledge the importance of the death rites and the anniversaries that follow. The Vedic traditions regarding the 13 days after death include helping the soul move on, so they are a type of deathwalking practice even if it isn't the same as the Western ones. To understand what the concept of death really is, we look to our Vedic scriptures. We do have a philosophical approach to death, but we also utilize symbolism through metaphors and analogies while conducting our rituals. Much of our mythology surrounding matters of death centers around the god Yama. He is considered the god of death in Hinduism, though his actual function can include many aspects.

There is a famous story from the Mahabharata involving Yama and a steadfast, headstrong young princess named Savitri. I had long heard this story growing up and even watched many films and television programs that depicted the tale. It was a story that focused on one woman's resolve and wits to go head-to-head with Yama himself. The story tells us that Savitri loved her husband deeply, and though she was warned that he would die within a year, she was determined not to let that happen. When Yama came to take her husband, the relentless Savitri refused to let him go and pursued Yama so far that he himself was astonished to see such willpower and strength. Yama then told Savitri that he'd grant her two wishes but that he would still take her husband. Savitri was quick on her feet and requested that her father-in-law be well for the first wish. Her second wish was for one hundred sons. Yama granted her wishes but realized soon that Savitri had tricked him. She was still married and could only have children through her husband. And that was how Savitri won her husband back from the clutches of death.

That was the story I grew up with throughout my childhood. I mention it because many legends and myths offer tales of journeying through the underworld or meeting a god of death or a god or goddess who ferries souls across. We often wonder what happens to the soul after we die. Where does the next chapter lead us after we cross over to the unknown, the great beyond?

In Hinduism, we believe that the soul reincarnates as per the law of karma. Karma states that whatever we did in our past lives determines the direction of the current life. There are also other beliefs, one of which is that whatever we think of or desire in our final moment of living will influence what we become or where we are born in our next life or lives. The process repeats. We are re-born until we attain moksha (salvation) wherein we no longer have any karma to burn off and therefore do not reincarnate.

Death is not seen as final but more as a stop sign. The rituals are designed to make the transitioning process easier but also to maintain our connection to the deceased. The body is typically cremated. In modern days, there is a faster process to cremation. But before, there was a funeral pyre. Afterwards, the ashes were scattered in the river, and if we were able to, we scattered them in the sacred river, the Ganges or Ganga. Rivers are significant and symbolic of life and death as they both have the power to give as well as take life and death away. The idea of scattering ashes to the river completes the cycle.

The final rites are often performed for the following major reasons: A) For the soul to move on. B) For the soul to leave the body swiftly and not linger. C) For the grieving process for the family. D) For the soul to reach the ancestors. These are just a few reasons but ones that I believe are the most important. The website *Hinduism Today* describes it as a voyage.

In the Hindu cosmology, the path to the afterlife is an epic journey that is influenced by the person's actions during life, but is also assisted by relatives in the days after the soul's departure. This belief, like others, varies across the vast Hindu world and can be understood on many levels. The soul's journey across the ghost-riddled plains and dangerous rivers of the Pretaloka (realm of the spirits) until it joins the ancestors in the Pitriloka (realm of the ancestors) can be seen as a literal voyage through alternate realms, as a symbolic envisioning of the process of death and rebirth, or as elements of both. Rites, like beliefs, also vary by family background, regional culture, community and devotional preference (Acharya, 2014).

My understanding is that the journey is symbolic. The stage in which we travel across various realms is sort of like an in-between. Reincarnating over and over is also like that. The final destination is liberation from the cycle of life and death. So why are death rites so important to us? Besides helping us cope with the grief that would naturally follow, they also give us a way to understand more about our own lives. The rites tie us to our lineage and ancestry and allow us to move on – with the belief that the deceased's last wishes before death are granted and/or they are reborn. That keeps them alive in our hearts and minds, knowing that the death of the body does not mean "gone forever."

The deceased is cremated so that the soul is not attached to the body and is able to leave the earthly plane faster. Typically, the 13 days of ritual begin after cremation. Sometimes, there is an active funeral before cremation in which the body is cleansed, dressed, and garlanded; mourners will view the body and say prayers or express grief here. Either way, the rituals are performed. During the first 10 days, an offering is made. The offering symbolizes each body part to complete the deceased's journey with Yama. The offering is usually a rice ball. It differs from family to family and region to region as well as varying sects. What I aim to provide here is a general description of Hindu death rituals and custom, and from my own understanding of what I was told growing up.

The eleventh day of ritual is to ensure the safe passage of the spirit or deceased's soul to the realm of the dead or ancestral abode. It is also known as shraddha. This ritual continues on after the 13 days on each monthly anniversary of death for the first year. "Bharatiya culture says that, just as we serve our parents and close relatives when they are alive as part of abiding by our Dharma, we have certain duties unto them after their death. The shraddha rites provide us with an excellent opportunity to fulfill these duties and repay our debts unto the pitars (ancestors)" (Sanatan Sanstha website). Here, Bharatiya culture refers to Indian Hindu culture, and Dharma is considered duty, more or less.

The twelfth day of ritual is to join the spirit with the ancestors. The thirteenth day completes the cycle in which the spirit reaches Vaikunta, the destination of the spiritual realm. Vaikunta is Vishnu's realm. We hope the soul reaches this realm because it is considered the ultimate destination of a liberated soul. That being said, while all these rituals are symbolic, we essentially give credence to life more so than death. Our current actions dictate our spiritual journey, and though Vedanta and

Hindu texts essentially discuss the non-duality of creator and creation, we do work symbolically within the world we transact with, and the gods and goddesses, rituals and customs are a means to realize that, as well as what we truly are. This is an account of my personal beliefs through family as well as what I have read. This is not a full discussion of final rites and customs but a brief overview.

Vani Neelakantan is a writer, singer, and English teacher with a background in literature, mythology, and ancient languages. Her passion for cultural understanding stems from having been born and raised in India for the first 10 years of her life. She is currently working on a young adolescent novel and doing some song writing in her spare time.

Dealing with Misplaced Energy: Examples and practices

Have you walked into a home or workplace and felt "something"? Has walking into a certain room made you feel tired or perhaps angry even? Have you noticed or felt someone or something shadowing you as you have been going about your daily routines? Has your workplace felt heavy or have doors opened or closed with no one visible? Have your friends noticed a distinct change in your behavior, or have you noticed this phenomenon in one of them? These and other similar symptoms may be indicative of a misplaced energy or spiritual intrusion.

In shamanism, there are only a few causes for dis-ease to manifest in our bodies or spirit, and spiritual intrusion is one of them. An intrusion of energy that does not belong to you can be a major discomfort, and will typically manifest with localized pain, changes in behavior or, in severe cases, a complete psychotic episode, depending on the nature of the intrusion. Although, by definition, an insect bite can be a spiritual intrusion, at the opposite end of the spectrum, the intrusion might present as a possession. Possessions can be complex, interesting and difficult, as the host may be affected deeply by the possessing spirit, and there are instances where the possessing spirit may not even realize that they are no longer in their own body, or that their presence may be harmful to the person that they are now inhabiting.

Not only people and so called living beings take on energies that are not their own. Buildings, lands, bodies of water, inanimate objects, or any being can attract and pick up an energy quite easily. If we consider that we are all energy, vibrating at certain frequencies, vibrations and frequencies that are external to the host can be drawn to the host like a magnet.

As we move through our day, we are touched by the energies

around us. Perhaps you have noticed that when you have driven down a busy street, filled with others trying desperately to get to work or home, that you might have begun to feel desperate, tense or angry. Is this your anger, or have you taken on the anger or desperation of those in the nearby cars? We are empathic beings, and for many, we are unaware of the intensity or power of our thoughts, emotions, and energy. Some people are aware of this power, however, and actually send energetic arrows at others. Let's consider the drive again: someone cuts in front of the car behind, and the driver of that second car raises his hand in anger. Without intending to, he may have sent the offending driver a bit of his anger. This anger may, over time, become a thought form within the recipient, causing dis-ease within.

We can be very irresponsible with our energy, sending out these little darts with or without awareness, causing discomfort in others, but making ourselves feel better, as we have released the offending energy.

Of course, our simple example of the angry driver might seem quite innocuous compared to driving past a fatal traffic accident or the site of a tragedy. For those who are sensitive or empathic, or even those who may not think that they are, these occurrences can affect us deeply. If we forget that we have choice, or are feeling vulnerable, ill, or perhaps weakened in some way, spirits that have left their physical bodies may literally float into a new host. Neither the host nor the lost spirit might be aware of this intrusion. The recently deceased may not be aware of their passing even, but have been drawn to a comforting place – within another being.

Some of those who have passed have difficulty fully transitioning, and find themselves "stuck" as spirits in this realm. These are the aberrations commonly referred to as ghosts or presences, and they may inhabit a familiar place, like the home they lived in on Earth, a building near the place they had their car accident, or even their place of work, to name a few.

They are unable, unwilling, or afraid to move forward to the home of their ancestors.

All these situations, from the angry driver to the possessing spirit, can be addressed in a similar manner. Please be sure to find a credible shamanic practitioner to assist with the healing that is required in your situation.

The first thing that a practitioner would perform is a diagnostic, assessing precisely what has occurred with the guidance of their spirit helpers. All practitioners have helping spirits who are working outside of time and space for the client's highest good. The client may be a person, a place, or an object, and the helping spirits will connect with this being and its helpers to determine the best possible course of action.

A house or building might feel heavy, or maybe a client is moving into a new home and wishes to have the energy cleared. In relatively simple cases, a practitioner would assess the need or intention and, using sacred herbs, plants, or resins, methodically move through the space performing what is known as smudging or clearing. This is an ancient practice using the smoke created from certain sacred herbs or plants such as sage or sweetgrass and/or sacred resins like copal or frankincense. The practitioner walks throughout the area, fanning the smoke with intention and prayer to clear unneeded or unwanted energy from the spaces that require it.

Smudging or clearing in this way is like taking a shower when our bodies are dirty – the smoke is like the water, washing the unclean energy from the space. It can also be used to clear a person or even an object, such as crystals or other sacred tools. As a practitioner, I smudge myself regularly. I also clear my drum, rattles, crystals, bowls, wands, pendulums and the like. During my regular work week, it is often necessary to clear my own energetic field, which I do frequently, as part of my own practice.

In my experience, when a person, space, place or object has

taken on energy that is not their own, helping spirits will begin the cleansing with a smudging, however, more will need to be done. The initial clearing may give clarity to the healing intention so that the rest of the work can be performed in the deepest and most compassionate way. Smudging sets sacred space in which to work. It is also imperative that the practitioner is very clear and filled with their most empowering light. Smudging can certainly help in this process.

It is so important that the practitioner is very clear about the work that they are doing once the diagnostic is complete and a healing is to commence. They must have a very good connection and rapport with their helping spirit. Indeed, there are usually specific healing spirits that will support this type of work through the practitioner. I have different helpers in every type of shamanic work that I conduct in my own healing clinic, and their appearance in the diagnostic journey is often the first clue as to which ceremony or healing work must be carried out. The relationship between the practitioner and the unseen is critical. The practitioner is a facilitator of spirit, and for their own protection, must be filled with light and healing energy, for the invasive energy that may be within their client may enter the practitioner if they are not adequately prepared. Preparation requires training, practice, and a strong intimate relationship with their helping spirits.

In the case of spiritual intrusion, the practitioner may use many tools for extraction. In listening carefully to guidance, I have been able to facilitate these healings using feathers, tuning forks, rattles, drums, eggs, my hands or mouth, or even using sounds like light language or toning. A receptacle for the misplaced energy is placed nearby; for instance a bowl of water, a candle, shell or crystal may be used to receive the unwanted intrusion, which will then be dealt with after the client leaves. There might be a burial of the egg that drew out the spiritual intrusion or a purification ceremony performed on the other tools. Whatever I am guided to do will take place, for it would be irresponsible to not follow through, perhaps even allowing a misplaced energy to escape and attach to someone or something else. There is a great deal of responsibility required in undertaking this work.

In dealing with the more complex intrusions, such as possessions or hauntings, the practitioner must be very aware of their abilities to listen to their guides, fill themselves with light, and have strong negotiating skills to deal with these spirits. I also feel very strongly that this work needs to be performed in a very compassionate and loving way. In my experience, the possessing spirit is usually very afraid and confused and requires great care to help them move to the next chapter.

Some people feel that possessing spirits are evil. I endeavor not to give them that much power. I choose to see them as frightened, and then I can support them through their transition in a compassionate and loving way. This work is known as psychopomping.

Certainly some possessing spirits appear evil. Some are extremely frightening! Our job as a practitioner is to hold our sacred space, including the sovereign self, in light and grace, and facilitate without fear. As we are working together, my helping spirits will indicate how to negotiate with the misplaced energy and encourage it to move toward its next step. Information about the cosmology or beliefs of the invasive spirit is typically brought through, so that it may transition accordingly. It has been my experience that a portal needs to be opened so that spirits may find their way home easily, but not all go without an argument or at least a discussion! As practitioners, we are offered ways for them to feel safe, loved, and supported on this important phase. Because this work is so intricate and potentially harmful, and because there was no intention for this chapter to go into specifics, I will leave the discussion at this.

During times of tragedy or disaster, communities, bodies of water, and areas of land can be invaded by lost spirits. Again, to heal these circumstances and send souls home requires diligence, competence, and compassion. I find that this work is often best performed with other practitioners or supporters, depending on the size of the area afflicted.

For example, in the case of an earthquake or other natural disaster, even if it is not close to where I live, I will ask for guidance from my helpers, who will connect with the area to establish both the permission to work there and the method of healing required. I have had wonderful results working remotely, either by myself or with others. When working with a group, we will typically find ourselves sitting in a spirit boat, traveling through time and space together, creating a safe portal for the trapped spirits to find their way home. A spirit boat or canoe is a boat-shaped formation of people with a clear intention, who travel together to the area to work.

We all have the right to sovereignty within our own being. This means that we do not need to allow any energy that does not belong to us to access our being. We must all remember that we have choice. If an intruding energy does try to gain access, if we are aware, we can say no. Once they are in us, we can choose to have them leave. Generally we will need help with that, but once the healing has been performed, we can remember to remain sovereign in our wholeness.

If you suspect that you or someone you know has energy in them that isn't theirs, if you feel that your home or office needs to be cleared, or if you wish to make more empowered and compassionate choices for a sovereign life, be sure to contact a shamanic practitioner to support you in your healing.

Janet Elizabeth Gale is a Shamanic Practitioner and Teacher, Usui and Karuna Reiki Master, Energy Healer, Acutonics Tuning Fork Practitioner, and certified Yoga Instructor. She has studied with Sandra Ingerman, Betsy Bergstrom, and Beth Berkins, as well as Gary Zukav and Linda Francis, and she holds a Doctorate of

Metaphysical Science. Her extensive studies have supplemented her hands-on work as she has deepened her understanding of spiritual empowerment and the creation of a life of trust and joy. She truly feels that to heal ourselves, our communities and our planet, we must embody a life that is supported by our connection with nature's spirits, the natural life cycles and the truth of who we are. Ms. Gale is the author of *The Rush Hour Shaman: Shamanic Practices for Urban Living.* You can find her online at sulishealing.com

Deathwalking: Three encounters with death

When I first met death, it wasn't what I expected.

I was a young witch then – well, in my 20s – and not very experienced. Even as I approach my 60s, with decades in the Craft, I would say that witches are not generally well trained for deathwalking. Although they should be. We will all encounter death sooner or later.

I was doing a meditation to meet the Goddess from *A Witch Alone: Thirteen Moons to Master Natural Magic*, Marian Green's excellent book for would-be witches. The meditation I was performing was to find out which Goddess I should be working with. I was expecting a lighter being, perhaps Epona or Brigit from Celtic mythology. In my mind's eye I followed a dark tunnel, not knowing where it would end. I was startled – even shocked – that what I saw when I emerged was a bloody battlefield covered with corpses and rotting heads. The battle had ended; all that was left was death. Above this, in front of me, was a figure, female, like a huge black bird of prey. I'll call her Death, because although all cultures give her a name, I would not want to restrict her to any one culture. And, yes, of course I was scared, but it faded. Death is not our enemy.

"You are not mine yet," was all she said to me. I was allowed to leave.

I met her again – or an aspect of her – several years later, as my friend died in my arms.

It was a Friday night in the 1990s and I was out clubbing with a group of friends. This was pretty normal; I was still young enough to rave all night and sleep all day as a regular weekend activity – and the friends I was with were my close clubbing buddies. Not that long after we arrived at the club, one of my friends said he felt unwell and wanted to sit down. I went with him, leaving our other friends dancing. Suddenly –

really completely without warning – he collapsed into my arms. I shouted for someone to get help. His heart had stopped, but someone trained in CPR got there fast and someone else called 999.

Everyone was trying to save him and everyone did all they could, but I knew he was leaving. Again, I saw that black bird of prey – smaller than before, but still large. I knew no one else could see the being. I wasn't sure if it was Death herself or a psychopomp. I wasn't scared that time – the Black Bird wasn't frightening. Somber, serene, the Black Bird quietly waited, hovering above my friend, despite all the noise, the activity of resuscitation, the pumping music and other clubbers who were still dancing and talking without realizing what was going on. I saw his spirit rise up out of his body and go towards Her.

"Please give him back," I pleaded.

I got a sense of implacability, of fixed purpose. No argument was possible.

"I have only come to speed his passing," said the Black Bird, and they left, my friend's spirit going with Her, down the long corridor out of the club and onwards. I knew my friend would not be revived, although those trying to do so didn't seem to realize it. The ambulance arrived, and all the way to the hospital they tried their best. Then the waiting at the hospital – all his friends, because we had all gone there with him. They told me I was being too pessimistic to say I knew he would not be returning to us. But I knew. I had seen him leave.

Could I have done more? I don't think so. I know my friend had had a hard life; perhaps he was ready for a better one. He had told me that as a young boy he had been abused by a priest and that he had never really gotten over that. Music and his close friends were the only things that made him happy. He had died in the place he would have wanted to be, with the people he would have wanted to be with. His death was by natural causes – a blocked artery causing a cardiac arrest. It was swift;

he hadn't suffered.

Of course it was a shock, and I grieved terribly, but I also knew that my friend's spirit had been guided onwards to the next life by one who knew the way. Many months later I got a message and knew his spirit was in a new place – a much better place – but that's another story.

Who could really ask more from Death?

Years later, I sat a death vigil for my father. He had gone into hospital for what should have been a routine knee operation, but contracted pneumonia and was in the hospital for a long time. I should probably add that my father was elderly and suffered from dementia. Before his operation, my mother – also elderly – had been his main carer, while my husband and I had recently given up our own flat and moved in with my parents to help them both.

With his illness he became even more confused, and out of this confusion refused to co-operate with the physiotherapists who were trying to mobilize him. He began to recover from the pneumonia, but it became apparent that he would never walk again and his dementia was getting worse. He became extremely aggressive, physically lashing out at the nurses and becoming very argumentative with his family when we visited him. During the time he was in this state in hospital, we gradually realized that when he came out we would not be able to care for him at home. Although at that stage, we had no reason to believe he would not come out of hospital alive.

Then, one evening, I visited him on the ward and he seemed a lot better; lucid and in a good mood. He told me how much he loved me and I told him I loved him, too. I had a chance to talk about various things from the past that needed reconciling. In hindsight, I know I should have realized people often have a lucid moment before they die. But I didn't.

I left feeling happier about his prospects than I had been for weeks. But then, in the early hours of the next morning, my family got a call from the hospital saying my father had lost consciousness. His pneumonia had returned. Further tests showed he had also contracted MRSA. They tried to save him, but he did not respond to treatment and did not wake at all. The MRSA was causing his organs to fail and, after several days, we were asked to make a difficult decision as to whether they should continue trying to save him – something that was not likely to succeed but would increase his discomfort – or whether he should be allowed to die in as much comfort as possible. We decided the latter.

The three of us – my mother, my husband, and I – conducted round-the-clock death vigils for him, staying there in 8-hour to 12-hour shifts on rotation. Days and nights went on like this. It felt as though we were all in some kind of limbo between life and death. A week went by.

I made a decision. I called on that Black Bird: Death, the psychopomp. The name didn't matter. I knew what She could do.

"Please," I said. "Please come and speed his passing."

And she did.

I've thought long and hard about the ethics of all the decisions I made during that time. Some were made by the family together after long discussion. That last one was made by me alone. I told my husband, later, afterwards. I never told my mother, and she is now with my father in death. I do not feel good about it, but I do know that if I was to relive that time, I would do the same again.

I know that one day I will die. I'm not afraid – not of death or Death. I'm afraid of pain and suffering, but death is just a transition. Sometimes people linger in pain and suffering – either in their bodies or in spirit – because they are scared of moving on. There is no need to be; it is part of the natural cycle of things. We all die and our bodies rot, like those bodies on the battlefield, but our spirits can move on, and it is best if they do so. When I am dying, I know that I will not want to linger. I will call on that Black Bird and whisper: "Please come to me. I am one of yours now. I am not afraid. Please, speed my passing."

I started my story by saying that in general witches are not well trained for deathwalking. I strongly believe that. Sure, some initiations involve a ritualized encounter with Death, but this isn't the same thing as actual training in how to help people as they face death, go into death and beyond. Deathwalking includes counseling the living in preparation for death as well as guiding the spirits of those who have died into the next realm either at the time of death or later if they linger in a way that is not helpful to them. In an untrained way, I dealt with situations that happened when I was present and no one else was around who could even see into the spirit realm. I probably made mistakes – that's usual when the untrained try anything for the first time without proper guidance – but I did my best. Shamanic practitioners have training in deathwalking as a core part of their learning. Us witches would do well to learn from them.

Lucya Starza is a Gardnerian Wiccan, although her current witchcraft practices are eclectic. She writes A Bad Witch's Blog, edited *Every Day Magic: A Pagan Book of Days* and is the author of *Pagan Portals – Candle Magic* and *Pagan Portals – Poppets and Magical Dolls*. You can find her online at A Bad Witch's Blog (www.badwitch.co.uk)

A Path of Song, a Path of Light: Guiding the dead in the Celtic traditions

Once, when our loved ones passed they were guided to the otherworld in a yearly ritual each *Samhain/Oiche Samhna/Nos Calan Gaeaf* (once Nov 7, now Oct 31) – an endless string of bonfires and lanterns, stretching out across the land to light their way. Known as tumpshies, these were carved turnips representing the spirits themselves, as a precursor to the modern pumpkin lantern. All the fires were extinguished and relit from the bonfire, and the lanterns were lit with these blessed flames to both scare away the unwanted dead and guide those who were loved on their way through the darkness. In Wales the spirits of the dead went to *Annwfn*, "the deep place" sometimes found across the sea, or beneath a lake, or within the land itself. In Ireland and Scotland, when someone died their spirits were carried to Tír na nÓg or any number of otherworldly destinations on a wave of song and ritual chants known as keening. Wearing veils and shawls to cover their faces, *"Na Caoineadh,"* the keening women, usually a main keener and two others, would gather at the "wake" or traditional funeral and lead the grieving party in ritualized weeping and wailing, and in the singing of ancient grief songs passed down through the years. Embodying the grief of the family and community, they encouraged others who may have found it hard, particularly the men in the family, to release their emotions and lose themselves in a flood of feeling ... trusting that this river of tears would carry both those left behind and the newly deceased towards healing and acceptance. Openly honoring their grief to the fullest extent was a healing act for both the soul of the departed and their loved ones.

"Na Caoineadh," the keening women enacted a sacred role of honoring the dead that was still commonplace in Ireland until the early twentieth century, but has its roots going back

millennia. Stone-chambered Neolithic burial or barrow mounds, found across Britain and Ireland and used to house the bones of ancestors, were ritual sites of profound importance to their communities. Here priests or shamans would perform seasonal rites of homage and propitiation for the souls of the dead, and perhaps also seek wisdom and advice from the ancestors on behalf of their tribe. What we know of these earliest death practices is that the bones of the dead were usually stripped of flesh, perhaps by excarnation – leaving the body out upon a high place for the birds to pick clean. Sometimes they were anointed with ochre, its red color most likely signifying the blood of life and the Earth itself, in a highly ritualized process. Later through the Bronze and Iron Ages, burials were performed with the body left whole, lain in the fetal position, as if returning for rebirth to the womb of the Earth, with ritual objects and tools of their living lives placed around them as both offerings and for their use in the otherworld or afterlife. Others were cremated and their ashes placed in womb-like vessels known as beakers. All burials were clearly highly ritualized and indicated a great degree of religious sophistication and committed belief.

A common thread among these practices is the theme of the Earth as a feminine entity and receptacle of the dead as well as the giver of life. This can be seen in the fetal position of Bronze and Iron Age burials and the physical structure of chambered tombs, often referred to as the *hollow hills* of faery in later tradition. These womblike enclosures were entered via a dark stone tunnel, its depths usually only penetrated by light at specific ritual times which coincided with the seasonal wheel of the year – most prominently the solar solstices and equinoxes. At Brú na Bóinne in County Meath, Ireland, for example, we see the depths of the back chamber illuminated by a single phallic ray of light at the dawn of the winter solstice, whereas West Kennet long barrow, part of the sacred complex at Avebury (Wiltshire, England) is aligned to and illuminated by the first rays of dawn on the spring and autumn equinoxes. Perhaps the spirits of the dead were released or revivified by these first rays of light. Not mere graveyards, these were places where the magic of life and death were enacted and the Earth as goddess was understood as both giving life and receiving the dead in equal measure.

We know in the later Celtic culture of the last few centuries, the preparation of the dead, like those attending childbirth, was predominantly a job for women. The myths and hero tales recorded in the medieval period, preserving far older oral lore, abound with examples of this ancient Earth goddess in varied lingering forms. She is found in Ireland in the Mórrígan, the bringer of death, and the *Ban Sidhe* or faery woman that howls and wails in a precursor to keening when death draws near. In Scotland she is also the *Bean Nighe*, the washer at the ford, endlessly washing the death shrouds and blood-stained clothes of those who are soon to cross over. She is the Cailleach, the old veiled one, the old woman of winter, of rock and stone, who lays out the dead and brings storms and knows the paths the soul takes into this life and from it, diving deep within her ever-churning cauldron. Yet she is also the giver of life, and in Ireland it is said that the very first keening of all came from Brighid, goddess of fire and life, goddess of midwives and new mothers, who sent out such a cry across the world when her son was slain.

So we see in the keening tradition that these weeping women hold a powerful liminal role, representing the goddesses of life and death and the thin sharp edge between the two. When our pagan past lay shrouded in the mists of time, these women still functioned ,in effect, as our indigenous priesthood, performing their sacred tasks regardless of the religious, usually Catholic, veneer that lay across their culture. It is not surprising that such a practice was often frowned upon and nearly died out across the early twentieth century, only to be passionately revived by the beginning of the twenty-first.

Not all the dead, however, were or are supported in their

journey to the afterlife, and in Wales and across Britain as well as much of northern Europe, it is the task of the Wild Hunt to ensure all lost souls, ghosts, and evil phantoms are swept from the land and taken to the Otherworld. In the Welsh Brythonic tradition, the Wild Hunt is led by Gwyn ap Nudd. Gwyn is a radiant god whose name means bright or light, and who is tasked with the guardianship of Annwfn, the Welsh underworld, later known as hell in the Christian tradition. Yet Annwfn, like those other Celtic Otherworlds preserved from pre-Christian oral lore, Tír na nÓg, Tír Tairngire, Mag Mell and others, is not a place of punishment or suffering. Annwfn is a miraculous place, where the everyday rules of society may be overturned and those who find its shores discover healing and transformation. Here according to traditional lore, the unwitting adventurer undergoes initiations and training at the hands of otherworldly women, talking animals, and magical cauldrons. Guardian and guide to those passing over, Gwyn functions as the quintessential Celtic psychopomp, who can be called upon to assist the passage of the dead or facilitate ancestral healing in his kinder aspects, but who also roams the wild winter skies shrieking and howling at the head of the ghostly hunt, bringing terror to fearful mortal souls and all those who would resist the cycles of life and death.

The Wild Hunt was often seen as a supernatural force that was invoked whenever great injustice occurred and upset the balance of society. In Britain, its earliest written account in 1127 sees it as a reaction from the spirit realm in response to the installation of an unsuitable abbot over a local community, yet it is a recurring motif across northern Europe and its roots are undoubtedly far more ancient than the written record. As a band of ghostly warriors and otherworldly spirits, they wreak havoc when they arrive unasked for, but remind the leaders of the community that the land itself must always be respected and there will always be forces beyond their control. The Wild Hunt can be called upon at times of national crisis, but also when psychopomp work demands greater forces in order to clear a site or move on a larger number of spirits who may resist their transition due to shock or denial, such as after war or a disaster. In such cases the Hunt is a mercy, seeing that no soul gets left behind, but is swept up in their irresistible chthonic current to their next destination.

Gwyn also oversees this transition of souls on a personal, individual level, and ensures that no walker between the worlds gets to access these inner sacred realms of the Earth goddesses without due testing, worth, and preparedness. Without the permission of the spirits and the gods themselves, no mere seeker may enter. To help those who cross over into death, on either side of the divide, is a sacred service, whether the soul is newly passing or centuries dead. Gwyn ensures all receive the compassion and protection they deserve.

Modern work in the Gaelic and Brythonic Celtic traditions may call upon all these deities and practices to help and serve this process, whether it is guiding a newly passed soul, or one hundred, whether it is to aid a trapped and unhappy or troublesome spirit or to seek the wisdom of a distant ancestor.

Call upon the Mórrígan to teach you wisdom and to understand the underbelly of the human psyche, and to bring peace after great discord or a traumatic death. She will teach you about finality and the deep currents of life and death. Call upon the Cailleach, the ancient one, to midwife the dying and the newly passed, and make prayers to her that she may hold their souls in her tender hands and transform them in her ancient cauldron. Call to Brighid when the time for death is passing, that she guides you from pain to healing, and brings the light back into your life, and transforms the dead and the grieving in her sacred fires. Call upon Gwyn when there are unquiet spirits that need leading onwards, when the pain of those who have passed traps them in-between the living and the dead. Seek his permission when looking for guidance in the underworld, and he will guide you to the wisdom you seek.

Ease the spirits' passing by telling their tales and feasting on their favorite foods, being sure to leave a portion for them upon the table at the traditional time of *Samhain/Oiche Samhna/Nos Calan Gaeaf*. Light a lantern, a tumpshie or a pumpkin, to guide the spirits to their rest when the wheel turns to winter, or someone passes, as a sign that they are remembered. Keep them in your awareness as they pass into spirit, and have a space set aside just for the ancestors, that they are woven into your life and you into theirs in an endless thread of healing and blessing. In this way your bloodlines may grow strong, with the prayers and support of the future generations healing those long passed ... as well as vice versa. And sing to them, sing to the dead. Let your grief, let your tears, and the longing ache of your love carry them to their distant shore ... let the heavens be rent to the sound of your laments, let the bones of your ancestors thrum in the earth to the rhythm of your songs, loud enough to carry them to the otherworld, and know that these bonds of love and care guide us on our way, from the first days till the last.

With thanks to my keening soul sisters in Ireland, Cait Branigan and Karen Ward of Slí an Chroí.

Danu Forest is a *Bean Feasa*, a traditional Wisewoman, and Celtic shaman as well as an *Ard BanDrui* (archdruidess) in the Druid Clan of Dana. She lives in the wild marshes surrounding the legendary Glastonbury Tor and is the author of several books including *Pagan Portals – Gwyn ap Nudd: Wild god of Faery, Guardian of Annwfn* and *Shaman Pathways – The Druid Shaman: Exploring the Celtic Otherworld*. For more information, courses, ceremonies and consultations including keening and psychopomp work, go to www.danuforest.co.uk

The How Not to Do It Chapter

We've all heard people make jokes about featuring in the "How Not to Do It" chapter of someone's book. Well, here I am, featuring *myself* of all people in just such a chapter, in an anthology that I'm editing. It's funny, but then again, it's not. Deathwalking is literally a deadly serious business, one that requires proper training for the safety of all concerned. So, I'm serving myself up as an illustration of how not to go about it. I hope you can learn from my example.

In order to explain how not to go about practicing deathwalking, I need to give you a little bit of background about myself. I won't go into any of the gruesome details, but I will warn you that I was abused as a child and I do have to mention some of that here. So bear with me for just a bit.

I'm going to tell you how I did it all wrong, but first I'd like to share one thing I managed to do mostly right. Quite by accident, at a very young age, I acquired a bunch of helpful and protective spirit guides. That's a very, very good thing. Anyone who does shamanic work needs helpers and protectors of the spirit sort. Just please acquire them in the usual manner, preferably with a good teacher assisting you, and not the way I did it.

How did it happen? During a particularly bad string of long days of abuse, I called for help. They answered. It really was that simple. But I have to be honest: I was very lucky that the ones who answered my call were the "good guys." That's not always the case; there are just as many self-serving, deceitful, and dangerous spirits as there are people. Maybe more. Believe me, I know. I've met some of them. That's why (and I'll say this over and over) you need proper training if you're going to do shaman-y things, to filter out the "bad guys." So again, I was lucky that the spirits who showed up for me were the helpful, friendly sort. They've been with me ever since, roughly fifty years now. It's a good thing, too, because otherwise I probably would have been dead long ago.

You see, one of the days when my mentally ill mother was especially rough with me, resulted in her giving me a concussion. I didn't know what a concussion was, of course; I was only four years old. I recognized the symptoms later on in life and was able to identify the injury. What I did know at the time was that my body was injured badly enough that I could leave it if I wanted to. And given my family situation, I think it's understandable that I wanted to leave. I remember thinking, "I can go now." The next thing I knew, I was standing on the bridge to the Otherworld with my hand on the Gate.

That Gate is a sort of one-way valve; you go through it and you're gone. I was standing there ready to open the Gate and step through it. I could feel the pull of Home, the place I'd come from, the place where truly unconditional love was, and I wanted it badly. Then those helpful, protective spirit guides showed up to talk me out of it. It took an awful lot of talking, but I'm still here, so obviously they eventually convinced me. Good thing, too.

Granted, I was seriously injured and had all sorts of reasons for wanting out of this life. But even perfectly healthy and happy people, when first confronted with the Gate, feel that draw, that heart-touching familiarity of the place we all come from and that we all eventually return to. This is so, so dangerous if you don't have a good teacher helping you and spirit guides keeping you safe and stable. It's terribly tempting to just walk through that Gate, and I've known a small handful of people who did just "walk off" when they discovered the Bridge and the Gate during untrained, unsupervised shamanic journeys. Or who left pieces of themselves there and had to have a lot of help to literally put themselves back together.

That concussion-induced near-death experience, if you want to call it that, was the introductory phase of my deathwalking career. About a year later, my great-grandmother died. She was a witchy sort herself, held in some degree of disdain and/or fear by most of the family. But she taught me a little bit of knot magic and was always kind to me, and I loved her. So I was confused when the adults told me she was gone, because I could see her clearly, hovering right over her casket there in the front room of her house (she was the last member of our family who was laid out at home).

She smiled at me and said, "Do you know where to go?" I knew she was talking about the Bridge and the Gate, so I nodded. "Good," she said. "Then go help that little girl." And then she was gone, crossing over quietly. I suspect she had her own spirit guides to help her make the journey.

"That little girl" was a girl in my neighborhood, about my age, who had recently died. When we got home, the next time I went out into the back yard, she was hovering over our fence. I told her about the Bridge and the Gate. In my mind, I showed them to her and assured her (with all the innocent confidence of a child) that was the right way to go. And so she went.

Over the years of my childhood I helped a handful of other people cross over. I wanted to help and there was no one I could talk to, no one who could tell me how to be a psychopomp (I had never even heard the term). I didn't really know what I was doing; all I knew was where the Bridge and the Gate were. I didn't know how to shield myself, how to set up buffers, how to ask my spirit guides to protect me and show me the right way.

In her chapter about children as psychopomps, Imelda Almqvist mentions that children who are traumatized are "opened up" in certain ways. That's exactly what happened to me. I had no boundaries, physical or energetic. So over the course of my childhood, I picked up some bits of unpleasant energy from some of the people I helped. Those energetic attachments did me harm on several levels and took a great deal of effort to clear away, years later when I finally knew what I was doing.

When I grew up and found the Pagan and shamanic

communities, I did eventually get some proper training in the techniques I had been using in slapdash fashion for so long. And that made all the difference. I'm thankful that I was able to cleanse and heal from the unprotected psychopomping I'd done as a child. So when my five-year-old daughter died in my arms, though I was overwhelmed with grief, I was also able to focus enough to make sure she crossed over safely. Holding the door open for her is probably the hardest thing I've ever done.

In the years since then, I've helped a number of people cross over, including a fundamentalist Christian aunt who was terrified that she had gone to Hell (because she didn't see literal angels playing harps and streets paved with gold) when, in fact, she hadn't even crossed over yet. I had to call on her brother, who had died the better part of a year earlier, to reassure her that she wasn't doomed and to help her move on. Then there was a friend's mother who was worried that her children weren't coping well with her sudden, unexpected death so she was hanging around when she needed to go on. Often, the deceased are concerned or confused in some way and need reassurance that it's all right to cross over. But, since they're only human (even if they're dead) they also have their problems and their energetic muck that can affect anyone who tries to help them.

Shamanic work, especially psychopomping, isn't easy. And it isn't always safe, either. It can be made safer with good training and supervision directly from a skilled teacher. Books are helpful; I won't argue that. I'm very glad you're reading this one. But there's no substitute for an actual teacher. Yes, in shamanism, ultimately our real teachers are the spirits. For the sake of your safety and sanity, though, I recommend checking out any or all of the programs listed at the end of the other chapters in this anthology. Each contributor has taken their own unique path in the world of deathwalking, and I bet one or more of them will ring your chimes.

I wish you well – and safe – in all your journeys, spiritual and otherwise.

Laura Perry is a Pagan author and artist. Her personal spiritual practice focuses on her ancestors and on Modern Minoan Paganism, both of which have substantial shamanic components. Her published books include *Ariadne's Thread: Awakening the Wonders of the Ancient Minoans in Our Modern Lives.* You can find her online at lauraperryauthor.com and leading the Facebook group Ariadne's Tribe.

Moon Books

PAGANISM & SHAMANISM

What is Paganism? A religion, a spirituality, an alternative belief system, nature worship? You can find support for all these definitions (and many more) in dictionaries, encyclopaedias, and text books of religion, but subscribe to any one and the truth will evade you. Above all Paganism is a creative pursuit, an encounter with reality, an exploration of meaning and an expression of the soul. Druids, Heathens, Wiccans and others, all contribute their insights and literary riches to the Pagan tradition. Moon Books invites you to begin or to deepen your own encounter, right here, right now.

If you have enjoyed this book, why not tell other readers by posting a review on your preferred book site.

Recent bestsellers from Moon Books are:

Journey to the Dark Goddess
How to Return to Your Soul
Jane Meredith
Discover the powerful secrets of the Dark Goddess and
transform your depression, grief and pain into healing and
integration.
Paperback: 978-1-84694-677-6 ebook: 978-1-78099-223-5

Shamanic Reiki
Expanded Ways of Working with Universal Life Force Energy
Llyn Roberts, Robert Levy
Shamanism and Reiki are each powerful ways of healing; together,
their power multiplies. *Shamanic Reiki* introduces techniques to
help healers and Reiki practitioners tap ancient healing wisdom.
Paperback: 978-1-84694-037-8 ebook: 978-1-84694-650-9

Pagan Portals – The Awen Alone
Walking the Path of the Solitary Druid
Joanna van der Hoeven
An introductory guide for the solitary Druid, *The Awen Alone* will
accompany you as you explore, and seek out your own place
within the natural world.
Paperback: 978-1-78279-547-6 ebook: 978-1-78279-546-9

A Kitchen Witch's World of Magical Herbs & Plants
Rachel Patterson
A journey into the magical world of herbs and plants, filled with
magical uses, folklore, history and practical magic. By popular
writer, blogger and kitchen witch, Tansy Firedragon.
Paperback: 978-1-78279-621-3 ebook: 978-1-78279-620-6

Naming the Goddess
Trevor Greenfield
Naming the Goddess is written by over eighty adherents and
scholars of Goddess and Goddess Spirituality.
Paperback: 978-1-78279-476-9 ebook: 978-1-78279-475-2

Shapeshifting into Higher Consciousness
Heal and Transform Yourself and Our World with Ancient Sha-
manic and Modern Methods
Llyn Roberts
Ancient and modern methods that you can use every day to
transform yourself and make a positive difference in the world.
Paperback: 978-1-84694-843-5 ebook: 978-1-84694-844-2

Readers of ebooks can buy or view any of these bestsellers by
clicking on the live link in the title. Most titles are published in
paperback and as an ebook. Paperbacks are available in traditional
bookshops. Both print and ebook formats are available online.

Find more titles and sign up to our readers' newsletter at
http://www.johnhuntpublishing.com/paganism
Follow us on Facebook at https://www.facebook.com/MoonBooks
and Twitter at https://twitter.com/MoonBooksJHP